INDIANAPOLIS UNION AND BELT RAILROADS

RAILROADS PAST AND PRESENT
GEORGE M. SMERK AND H. ROGER GRANT, EDITORS

INDIANA UNIVERSITY PRESS

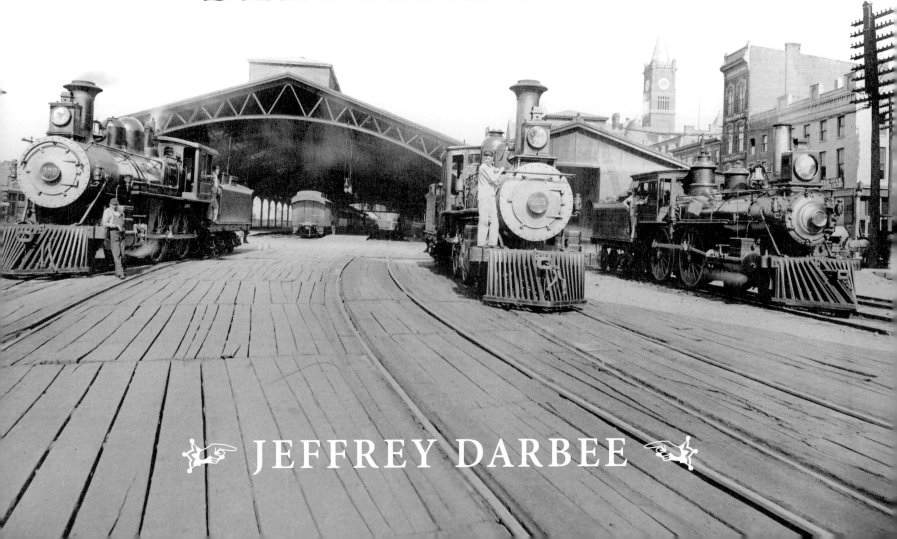

INDIANAPOLIS UNION
and
BELT RAILROADS

JEFFREY DARBEE

This book is a publication of

Indiana University Press
Office of Scholarly Publishing
Herman B Wells Library 350
1320 East 10th Street
Bloomington, Indiana 47405 USA

iupress.indiana.edu

Manufactured in the United States of America

Library of Congress
Cataloging-in-Publication Data

Names: Darbee, Jeffrey T., author.
Title: Indianapolis Union and Belt Railroads /
Jeffrey Darbee.
Description: Bloomington, Indiana : Indiana
University Press, [2017] |
  Series: Railroads past and present | Includes
bibliographical references
  and index.
Identifiers: LCCN 2017023769 (print) | LCCN
2017004830 (ebook) | ISBN
  9780253029508 (eb) | ISBN 9780253025227
(cl : alk. paper)
Subjects: LCSH: Indianapolis Union Railway
Company. |
  Railroads—Indiana—Indianapolis—
History. | Railroad
  travel—Indiana—Indianapolis—History.
Classification: LCC HE2791.I53 (print) | LCC
HE2791.I53 D37 2017 (ebook) |
  DDC 385.09772—dc23
LC record available at https://lccn.loc.gov
/2017023769

1 2 3 4 5 22 21 20 19 18 17

CONTENTS

PREFACE

From successive generations of Americans the railroad has exacted an almost universal fascination. It is not difficult to understand why this has been so. Prime mover in the civilization of a continent and the building of a nation, and, in its time, the indispensable mover of goods and purveyor of personal transportation, the railroad wove a net of steel rails that bound America together and brought a breath of far and fascinating places to the most commonplace of lives. Touching every life, the railroad could not be ignored.

Even more captivating, perhaps, has been the sheer physical impact of the sound and sight of massive machinery in motion that the railroad brought close to hand in a manner totally unlike any other industry. Shrieking, clanging, roaring, and pounding its way through town and countryside, the railroad embedded itself in the subconsciousness of every American; one could never be indifferent to its presence.[1]

WITH THESE WORDS, the late William D. Middleton, rightly considered among the top occupants of the pantheon of railroad historians, opened his sweeping yet very personal pictorial look at the vast drama of American railroading in the two and a half decades that followed the end of World War II. Through his photography Middleton showed railroads north, south, east, and west—all across the nation—doing their jobs in summer and winter, day and night, city and country. More than just pictures of the trains themselves, the images in his book placed each railroad in context by including the bridges, depots, yards, and landscapes that defined it. And, not least, Middleton made a point of including the people who made the trains run, typically with each individual's name, in many of the photographs.

The 144 pages of that book do indeed capture the "big picture" of American railroading in a very compelling way, and the author's focus on placing the railroad in context is a large part of its appeal. Intriguing as the "shrieking, clanging, roaring, and pounding" denizens of the rails can be, the broader story of the railroad's unique place in American history is at least as compelling.

Sometimes a part of that story can be told with a very narrow focus. I am one of Middleton's people, those whose life the railroad has touched; I am not indifferent to the railroad, and I cannot ignore it. A lifetime filled only with the study of railroads and their history would be enough for me. At the same time, a long career in historic preservation and urban history has led me to ask questions about the interplay of the railroad and the cities and villages it served, particularly how each helped to shape the other.

I am by no means the first to consider this question; books such as John R. Stilgoe's *Metropolitan Corridor*, Carl W. Condit's *The Railroad and the City*, and Joseph P. Schwieterman's *When the Railroad Leaves Town* have all tackled the subject. Each does so with a different focus—Stilgoe's view was broad; Condit focused on Cincinnati, Ohio; and Schwieterman looked mainly at smaller communities. All of these studies, and I am sure many more of which I am unaware, have contributed to a better understanding of the complex relationship between the railroad and the places it served.

When I was given the chance to study two small railroads in one particular city, I first focused on the railroads themselves—the Indianapolis Union Railway and the Indianapolis Belt Railroad—and the main-line railroads they served, the Union for passenger traffic and the Belt for freight. I soon found maps showing these railroads in detail and in relation to the street patterns of Indianapolis. Knowing that the historic 1888 Indianapolis Union Station was and still is at the heart of the city's railroad nexus led me naturally to ask what role those railroads and that landmark building had played in the shaping of this important midwestern community and also what role the city—its physical form, its politicians and business interests—had played in shaping the local railroad network and facilities. The deeper my research went, the more interested I became in trying to make my own contribution to the published record on this admittedly somewhat arcane aspect of our nation's history. I hope I have succeeded and that this book will inspire others to ask the same questions in their own communities.

ACKNOWLEDGMENTS

MY NAME IS on the cover of this book, but it's there because a whole army of helpful people made it possible. Many other authors have said this, but it is as true as ever: I could not have done it without them.

My thanks go first to Thomas G. Hoback, founder of the Indiana Rail Road (INRD), who conceived the idea of a book on the Indianapolis Union (IU) and the Belt and sponsored my efforts. He also showed admirable patience during a long research and writing process. Other helpful INRD people, current and former, include Robert Babcock, Shae LeDune, and Larry Ratcliffe. Eric Powell of INRD took me on a daylong, frigid, but informative tour to places where we could (safely) view the Belt of today.

My thanks also to the Railway and Locomotive Historical Society (R&LHS), which awarded me the first annual William D. Middleton Research Fellowship in 2012. Robert F. Holtzweiss, president, and Paul Gibson, treasurer, were most generous in awarding this support at a critical time. Thanks also to Mark Entrop of R&LHS for encouraging me to apply for the Middleton Fellowship.

Leigh Darbee and Robert Barrows, my sister and my brother-in-law, were always gracious in giving me a place to stay during my trips to Indianapolis. Both are published historians, and Leigh was of great help in tracking down images at the Indiana Historical Society library. Some of their published work helped me tell the IU and Belt story.

The Indiana Historical Society's William H. Smith Memorial Library was a treasure trove of primary and secondary sources, as well as excellent historical images. My thanks to Suzanne Hahn, vice president, Archives and Library; Steve Haller, former senior director, Collections and Library; Nadia Kousari, coordinator of visual reference; Dorothy Nicholson, archivist, Manuscript and Visual Collections; and Susan Sutton, director of digitization.

Brian Banta, railroad archives collector par excellence, lent a large amount of IU Railway material and trusted me with it for an extended period. Thanks, Brian.

Wayne Maple of Train Central in Indianapolis helped early on by providing names and phone numbers of knowledgeable Indianapolis railroaders, photographers, and collectors, all of whom were of great help in assembling information. They include Richard K. Baldwin, whose railroad archive is better organized than just about any other I have seen; he was a generous host during several visits who let me copy and scan important materials. Gene Maresca and John Ricci met with me to provide original documents and photos. Danny Walker, former IU Railway signalman, provided firsthand insights, as did Bob Wheeler and Tom Bonsett, whom I reached through the group Railfans of Indianapolis. Jim Tremblay, the Indianapolis Union Railway's superintendent and auditor until the folding of IU into CSX, provided information and perspective.

Mary K. Geary of the Transportation Library, Northwestern University, guided me through that fine collection. Monique Howell, reference librarian, Indiana Collection, Indiana State Library, provided maps from the state's collection. Bill Howes, of the Lexington Group in Transportation History and the Railway and Locomotive Historical Society, tracked down an early news item about Union Depot. The Indianapolis Public Library was helpful in providing access to its map collection. Barry Lafever and Craig Presler found large historical maps for me. Monica Schwarz, senior contract administrator, RM Acquisition, LLC, assisted me in making use of the 1918 Rand McNally Commercial Atlas map of Indianapolis.

Although they are credited in the image captions, I especially want to thank Bob's Photos, John Fuller, Gary Rolih, and Jay Williams for providing many of the book's photos. My son, James Darbee, was of great help in scanning many of Dick Baldwin's photos and other materials. Aaron Blevins gave me invaluable assistance in improving the quality of numerous image scans.

Bill Metzger, whom many will recognize from his excellent work in the books and magazines put out by Kalmbach Publishing Co., made the maps that are so helpful in visualizing the IU and the Belt over the years.

I took long enough completing this project that I have worked with three former and current Indiana University Press editors: Linda Oblack, Sarah Jacobi, and Ashley Runyon, all of whom have been patient and helpful.

H. Roger Grant, the Kathryn and Calhoun Lemon Professor of History at Clemson University, reviewed the manuscript and provided very helpful information and comments. He also has led the Lexington Group for many years, and the Grant Administration has so far remained scandal-free. Thanks, Roger.

Then there is my patient wife, Nancy Recchie, who kept me going until the work was done. My better half for sure. Thanks, Nancy. We are definitely a team.

As any author fears, I may have failed to note everyone who assisted me in this work. If so, my sincere apologies and my thanks. And, finally, I would note that, although I have learned a great deal about Indianapolis and its railroads, I am by no means an expert on the subject. I have tried to be careful in verifying factual information, but I take responsibility for any errors and would welcome any corrections.

INTRODUCTION

THIS BOOK DISCUSSES the development of the steam railroads of Indianapolis and how they affected the urban form and character of the city, but the focus is on the two smallest ones: the Indianapolis Union Railway and the Indianapolis Belt Railroad. A basic resource for any railroad historian is *The Official Guide of the Railways and Steam Navigation Lines of the United States, Porto Rico, Canada, Mexico, and Cuba.* That being something of a mouthful, if one refers simply to the *Official Guide,* others in the railroad field, at least, will know of which one speaks. This "bible" is still published today as the *Official Railway Guide* and remains an important reference in the field of transportation and logistics. For historians, however, it is the trove of monthly issues, going back well over a century, which brings the past to life. The *Official Guide* is always a good place to start when researching the history of any given railroad.

Selected at random, the July 1963 *Official Guide* has the following entry among the fourteen railroads that appear on page 47:

INDIANAPOLIS UNION RAILWAY CO.
OPERATING
UNION PASSENGER STATION. UNION TRACKS.
INDIANAPOLIS BELT RAILROAD.

Following a list of general officers, the entry notes, "Line owned, 1.72 miles; line leased (Indianapolis Belt), 14.16 miles; total miles operated, 15.88. Locomotives, 12. This is a Co-operative Terminal Road providing terminal facilities and doing a switching business for the roads entering Indianapolis."

The IU Railway's entry in the *Official Guide* for June 1916 is, except for the corporate officers and modest differences in mileage and number of locomotives, exactly the same—the same wording, the same punctuation, and almost the same typefaces.

To people who sometimes go whole days without thinking about railroads, these notations in musty, long-out-of-date volumes would mean little. To others, they whet the appetite to know more. There are so few words in those entries, yet they communicate so much: corporate names, corporate relationships, names of important officers, mileage, locomotive fleet, services provided. Any of these could be a jumping-off point for further inquiry. Measuring no more than about two by three inches, the entries were far too small to include a map, but there is always a map available somewhere—in atlases, ICC valuation records, Sanborn Map Company fire insurance maps, city maps of all kinds and dates, railroad records, and in the archives of collectors of all things railroad.

So, what was the Indianapolis Union Railway? The two historically dominant railroads of the Midwest and the Northeast—the Pennsylvania and the New York Central—came to be the owners, lessees, and/or operators of eleven of the sixteen rail routes that radiated from the Hoosier State's capital city. The New York Central had six of those routes, the Pennsylvania five. Of the remaining five, two were under the aegis of the Baltimore & Ohio, and the Norfolk & Western, the Illinois Central, and the Monon claimed one each. These roads would shape the rail map of Indianapolis, and for half of the nineteenth and most of the twentieth century they would also be a major factor in the shape, look, feel, and economic destiny of the city itself.

Those railroads and their various predecessors were the main players, but they could not have functioned as they did without the two little roads that connected them all. Though small in size, the Union and the Belt had an outsized impact, both on the city's rail network and on the city itself, due to their early construction dates and their locations: a half mile south of Monument Circle in the case of the Union and, for the Belt, a U-shaped alignment with a radius of just under two to just over two and a half miles from the Circle. Within that tight geographic area, a web of steel rails would grow over a half century and become integrated into the physical fabric of Indianapolis. The Union and the Belt, like the main lines with which they connected, would grow and then contract over time in response to economic conditions and changes in transportation technology. Their original corporate forms ceased to exist long ago, and physically not much is left of them today. Even so, they are still there, and they have intriguing histories, not the least part of which is how they showed the way for other cities seeking to manage their railroad networks. It is a unique story worth telling.

NOTE

1. William D. Middleton, *The Railroad Scene* (San Marino, CA: Golden West Books, 1969), 6.

INDIANAPOLIS UNION AND BELT RAILROADS

1

EARLY INDIANAPOLIS: SETTLING "THE WEST"

BEFORE THE UNITED STATES achieved independence from England, the lands west of the Appalachian Mountains were largely unknown, but with the end of the Revolutionary War in 1783 constraints upon westward expansion were gone and land-hungry easterners began to move. For many of them, the new United States, which had recently been thirteen British colonies, was simply too crowded, but another imperative was also at work: the promise that a free society and a vast land would offer wealth and success to anyone willing to seize opportunity and work. It was seen as a birthright of Americans that they should take up and settle the entire North American continent.

Presidential historian Doris Kearns Goodwin, quoting French writer Alexis de Tocqueville, summarized this driving force: "The idea of progress comes naturally into each man's mind; the desire to rise swells in every heart at once, and all men want to quit their former social position. Ambition becomes a universal feeling."[1] Western lands proved irresistible to a people convinced of their right to prosperity.

The challenge was to get there. The Great Lakes, the Ohio River, and the Mississippi River—along with some tributary waterways—were natural pathways by which most early settlers moved into the area. Yet these routes left much interior land out of reach, or accessible only by dangerous and time-consuming overland journeys. Even in the eighteenth century it was axiomatic that development followed extension of transportation routes: George Washington worried about this and about competition for development of the West. "Open wide a door and make a smooth path for the produce of that Country to pass to our markets," he is quoted as saying, "before the trade may get into another channel."[2] The Spanish at that time held lands west of the Mississippi as well as the busy port of New Orleans, and Washington feared that they or other powers might take permanent hold of large parts of North America. Transportation had both economic and geopolitical implications.

DIVIDING UP THE LAND

To ensure orderly western settlement, Congress adopted the Land Ordinance of 1785 to govern the sale of public land in the Northwest Territory, the region bounded by the Ohio River, the Mississippi River, and the Great Lakes. Congress wanted to avoid conflicts arising from archaic survey methods using as land parcel boundaries trees, buildings, objects, or landowners' names, all of which changed over time. The ordinance established the Rectangular Survey System (also called the Public Land Survey System), tested in the late eighteenth century on the eastern flank of what would become Ohio. It was a cadastral survey system, with land parcel boundaries recorded in an official register so they could be easily ascertained. The rectangular system used fixed markers, careful surveying, and precise boundary lines so that any land parcel could have a discrete, standardized description. Land was laid out in divisions called townships that were intended to reflect, roughly, the basic political subdivision in New England. Each township was six miles on a side, thirty-six square miles in area.[3] Each square mile, containing 640 acres of land, was called a section. Sections could be subdivided into quarter sections of 160 acres, and these could be further divided into "quarters of quarter sections," which contained 40 acres each.[4] Vertical rows of townships, called "ranges," were numbered with Roman numerals, and each township in a range was numbered with an Arabic numeral. (Township names came later, after settlement began and counties were established.) Within each township, the sections were numbered 1 through 36 in an east–west zigzag pattern. The legal description for a 40-acre plot, then, might read, "Range III, Township 4, the southwest quarter of the northeast quarter section of Section 18." Confusing at first glance, this was actually a very precise description of a land parcel and its location.[5]

The new system greatly facilitated western settlement. Some thirty states eventually were surveyed in whole or in part by the Rectangular Survey System, and its influence is readily visible today in the "checkerboard" pattern of farm fields, roads, tree lines, and fences, especially west of the Mississippi. Any air traveler can easily pick out sections, quarter sections, and quadrants of quarter sections in rural areas. The traditional "grid" pattern of cities and villages in much of the nation was largely a result of this method of surveying.

Indiana Statehood

By the end of the eighteenth century native tribes in the Old Northwest (over time this became the popular name for the Northwest Territory) had been subjugated and forced to move westward, opening the region to white settlement. Ohio was the first state to be formed, and on March 1, 1803, it became the seventeenth star on the national flag. But for Louisiana, admitted to the Union on April 30, 1812, Indiana would have been next. It did, however, become the nineteenth star on December 11, 1816. Settlement dated as far back as the 1730s, and the Indiana Territory was formed in 1800. Its name is said to have been "a coined name presumed to mean 'land of the Indians.'"[6] It took another thirty-two years to establish the other three states carved out of the Northwest Territory: Illinois on December 3, 1818; Michigan on January 26, 1837; and Wisconsin on May 29, 1848. The last bit of the territory, at its far northwestern tip, became part of the thirty-second state, Minnesota, in 1858.

Establishment of Indianapolis

The "Land of the Indians" was still young and raw when the federal government gave it four square miles of wild and heavily

Figure 1.1 An undated engraving depicts what many people even today think of Indiana: flat, open prairie dotted with small stands of trees. This was never entirely true, of course, and especially not today, but the "land of the Indians" did have a topography generally favorable for settlement. And the place certainly was flat enough to encourage the rapid spread of the railroads that would become a defining feature of the landscape.

Indiana Historical Society, P0211

Engraved by E. Teel from the Original Painting by George Winter.

PRAIRIE SCENE, INDIANA.

Engraved Expressly for the Ladies' Repository.

WESTERN CLEARING.

4

Figure 1.2 Titled Western Clearing, this early engraving embodies all the elements of homesteading in the western wilderness: the rude log house in a small stump-filled opening in the forest; the omnipresent campfire and cooking pot; plentiful game that regularly graced the dinner table; and men at work "girdling" trees to kill them off so more land could be cleared for crops. The promise of land, freedom, and opportunity drove people west and enabled them to endure the hardships of early settlement.

Indiana Historical Society, P0211

timbered land just east of the White River on which to build its capital. These 2,560 acres were bounded by the "Donation Line," a square two miles on a side defining the form of the proposed city. The person chosen to plat the new community, Alexander Ralston (1771–1827), was a Scottish surveyor and engineer who was engaged with Englishman Elias Fordham to prepare the plat of Indianapolis, which means "the principal city of Indiana."[7]

In 1821 the surveyors platted a 640-acre section, the "Mile Square," and created a regular grid-pattern town that was a child of the rectangular system. Landscape historian J. B. Jackson, in his 1970 book *Landscapes*, quotes historian John Reps as stating that "a great majority of American towns started and grew on the grid plan because of the ease of its layout in surveying, its simplicity of comprehension, and its adaptability for speculation."[8] "Adaptability for speculation" presumably meant that grid-surveyed lots were easy to locate, describe, subdivide, or combine for real estate ventures. Geographer James Vance noted that speculation did drive the emergence of an American urban form, with William Penn's plan for Philadelphia as a model: "Only the Philadelphia model was at all original, and then mainly in the

vast scale of its speculative expectations. . . . It remained for the children of those original settlers to develop the land, and to do so they had to Americanize the European city forms. The first effort along that line came with the elaboration and extension of the Philadelphian speculator's town. In Pittsburgh, Cincinnati, Louisville, and Columbus before 1825, this regularly parceled form, with its multiplicity of easily described lots that might be sold at a distance, took on a finished form."[9] Vance did not mention Indianapolis, but he did include it on a map as an example of the "Philadelphia model."

Jackson's book also notes that not all American communities were strictly "grid" in form: "But aside from one or two notable exceptions—Detroit, Baton Rouge, and Indianapolis—the cities built in the United States until late in the nineteenth century all conformed to the grid system."[10] There were efforts to "break the grid," to do town planning more in tune with the landscape. For example, Frederick Law Olmsted, designer of New York City's Central Park, in the early 1870s was hired to plan the city of Tacoma, Washington Territory. He ignored the traditional grid for the hilly site and planned curving streets across slopes, irregular

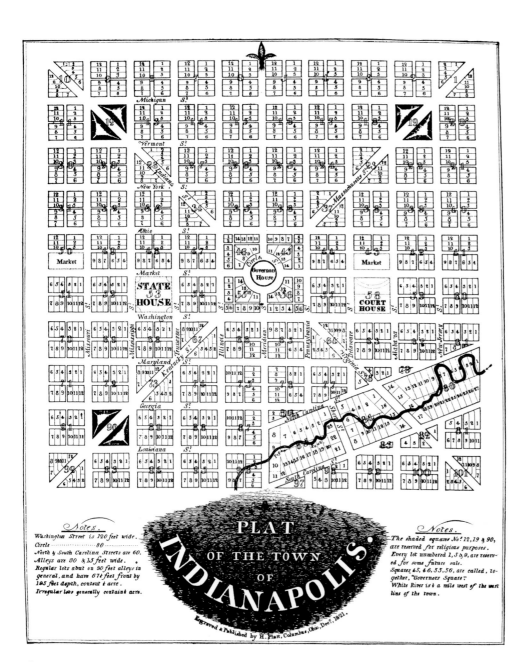

Figure 1.3 The 1821 Ralston plat of Indianapolis was shaped by two early-nineteenth-century town planning influences: the Rectangular Survey System, which divided public lands into easily surveyed and precisely defined rectangular parcels, forming the now-familiar urban grid pattern; and, as in Washington, DC, and a few other places, the use of diagonal streets that helped to break up that grid. It would take a while, but, contrary to Ralston's opinion, Indianapolis would grow far beyond this original Mile Square.

Indiana Historical Society, Bass Photo Co. Collection

lot shapes and sizes, and a waterfront park. The client was less than enthusiastic: "The most fantastic plat of a town that was ever seen. There wasn't a straight line, a right angle or a corner lot. The blocks were shaped like melons, pears, and sweet potatoes. One block [was] shaped like a banana. . . . It was a pretty fair park plan but condemned itself for a town."[11] So much for creative town planning. The purpose of laying out cities, darn it, was to sell land and fill it up; none of this fancy stuff. So in most places there was not much variation from the conventional, profitable grid.

However, there were those "one or two exceptions" mentioned by Jackson. What they shared—and there were at least three exceptions, or four if Buffalo, New York, is counted—was an overlay of diagonal streets. Moving off the grid with straight but angled streets was European in origin and French in particular. Even before the transformation of Paris in the second half of the nineteenth century, urban planners were introducing wide boulevards, open public squares, and building sites at points where diagonals and the grid intersected. In the United States, this idea is best represented by Washington, DC, whose diagonal boulevards and public circles and squares are its most distinctive feature. Its designer was Pierre L'Enfant, a French-born American who served on the side of the colonies in the war for independence. Detroit and Baton Rouge, though of more modest scale, had similar forms. They were eighteenth-century French settlements with the same kind of asymmetrical diagonal avenues as Washington. Buffalo had them, too. It was a Dutch settlement of the late eighteenth century, its form likely influenced by diagonal streets in cities such as Rotterdam and Amsterdam.

Indianapolis was not a French or Dutch colonial settlement, but surveyor Ralston had worked with L'Enfant in Washington and brought the same ideas to central Indiana. Reckoning that the new capital city would never fill up the four square miles granted to the state, Ralston surveyed and platted only the Mile Square, imposing his own concepts to create a distinctive symmetrical plan within the strictures of the rectangular system. This patch of wilderness was set out as ten blocks by ten blocks with a pattern of evenly spaced streets and twelve uniformly sized building lots in each block. Intra-block alleys formed four groups of three lots each.[12] The primary streets were Meridian, which ran north–south along the 86th meridian of longitude, and Market, named for the two public venues to be built along it. The radiating diagonal streets, Massachusetts to the northeast, Virginia to the southeast, Kentucky to the southwest, and Indiana to the northwest, all today are called avenues rather than streets. These public ways put Indianapolis in the realm of European city planning: many lots were triangular and trapezoidal and when filled with buildings gave the city unusual urban vistas and a distinctive built environment. Full blocks were set aside for a statehouse and a courthouse, three others for religious purposes, and halves of two lots along Market Street for the public markets. Circle Street, intersected by Meridian and Market, was the only non-linear street on the plat and encircled a central lot designated for the Governor's House; the Soldiers and Sailors Monument stands there today.[13]

One other notable exception illustrated the fact that overlaying a fixed grid on the natural landscape did not always result in a perfect pattern of streets and lots. Irregularities of the landscape sometimes dictated how land was platted, in many cases forcing changes in the grid (a fact that Olmsted certainly knew). This was the case in Indianapolis, where, in the southeastern portion of the

Figure 1.4 It is doubtful whether in 1825 Washington Street in Indianapolis was marked by a sign nailed to a tree. If such a sign did exist, it represented the optimistic view of the city's early settlers that the stump-strewn thoroughfare would one day become a real roadway. In fact, that optimism was borne out by the coming of the National Road along Washington Street not many years later. However, this view does illustrate the vicissitudes of overland travel in those early years.

Indiana Historical Society, Bass Photo Co. Collection

plat, Pogue's Run (also written as Pogues Run)[14] took a generally southwestern course on its way to the White River. The lots here were tilted nearly 45 degrees to the grid and at right angles to the run; this allowed the maximum number of lots with water frontage. The area was bounded on the north and south by streets cleverly named after North Carolina and South Carolina and on the east and west by East and Meridian streets. This formed a parallelogram-shaped plat that was crossed by Virginia Street and the aptly named Short Street and that contained several dozen building lots. Ralston presumably intended this area as

an industrial district, hence each lot's access to water. Disruption of the grid along Pogue's Run resulted in the insertion of an eleventh block in the ninth row, giving Ralston's plat 101 city blocks.[15]

Indianapolis illustrated a common characteristic of American town development. Because watercourses could be both a water supply and a convenient sewer, the more "upstream" land parcels quickly became more desirable and valuable, while the "downstream" parcels, where a regular flow of sewage and offal was common, were less attractive and of lower value. So prime residential areas generally were upstream, and less wealthy

Figure 1.5 Indianapolis exists because it was designated as the capital of Indiana (the designation came first, then the town). Indiana has had five statehouses, the first in Corydon and the others in Indianapolis. This was the third statehouse, built in 1835 and used until 1876, when the General Assembly vacated the deteriorated building. State government occupied a converted office building until completion of the fifth and current statehouse in 1888. This scene shows that the Hoosier wilderness so visible in early engravings had been quite thoroughly tamed.

Indiana Historical Society, P0211

residents, along with various commercial and industrial enterprises, typically were consigned to downstream areas. Because of the general direction of flow of midwestern creeks and rivers, the north sides of most communities tended to be the most desirable.

THE PROBLEM OF TRANSPORTATION

Before Indiana and the other states of the Old Northwest could begin sustainable economic development, one serious issue had to be addressed: writing in 1912, Frederic L. Paxson noted that "transportation, after all, has determined both the course and the period of Western development; and in no section of the continent has this determination been more nearly absolute than in the region between the Ohio River and the lakes."[16] Well into the nineteenth century, getting "out west" to seek one's fortune was difficult. Established water routes took people around the edges of the region; some interior rivers were navigable but varied in depth and in many cases were too shallow for any craft other than a canoe. Reaching the interior had to be by foot along animal or Native American trails through forests and open prairie over

N.T. Russell Smith.

George H. Cushman.

Scene on the Ohio.

Printed by D. Stevens

Figure 1.6 Many early settlers reached Indiana by means of an ancient water highway: the Ohio River. In this romantic scene, an open flatboat navigates the broad, empty, and seemingly placid waterway; but a closer look at the riverbank reveals a band of men, presumably hostile native tribesmen, firing rifles at the settlers. This early form of inland travel could be anything but idyllic.

Indiana Historical Society, P0211

many days or weeks; and bringing in supplies and shipping out produce and other goods was a major problem.

River and Lake Travel

Early lake and river watercraft were human- or sail-powered, and sometimes both. Up to about 1820, these included flatboats, pirogues, canoes, keelboats, rafts, sloops, and other craft of myriad shapes and sizes, and they did facilitate settlement and at least rudimentary economic development. At the same time, they had the obvious limitations of slow speed, low carrying capacity, labor intensity, and seasonal unavailability. Steam power's practicability was proven by the travels in 1811 of the steamer *New Orleans* on the Ohio and Mississippi rivers, and steam-powered craft quickly became a common sight. By the 1850s, for example, Cincinnati would record some eight thousand steamboat arrivals and departures in a single year.

Indiana historians have noted the difference in economic advantage that tended to accrue to settlements along water routes: "Some three dozen Indiana towns had been established on the Ohio River by 1830, including New Albany and Madison, then the state's two largest. Ten years later, over four-fifths of the state's residents lived in the southern half of the state, and one-half of those lived within seventy-five miles of the Ohio River. . . . Ten of the thirteen Indiana counties that touch the Ohio River have county seats situated on the river rather than in the interior. And of the fourteen counties touched by the Wabash, ten have their seat of government adjacent to the river."[17]

However, even though it was the state capital, Indianapolis lacked navigable waterways and was destined to live without river transportation, despite initial high hopes. Attempts to serve the city by steamboat all were doomed to failure, symbolized by the *Robert Hanna*, a steamer named for a National Road contractor who used his vessel to bring road-building supplies to Indianapolis. The *Hanna* arrived safely in April 1831 but ran aground on its downstream run and was stranded long enough to scotch any dreams of river travel.[18]

Trails, Turnpikes, and Roads

So Indianapolis would have to rely on land transport. The state legislature in 1821 launched construction of a series of "state roads," ten in all, intended to link Indianapolis with other parts of Indiana.[19] Two roads in particular, one state-built and the other federal, were of great importance in both establishing Indianapolis as the center of transportation in the state and spurring the development of trade and commerce northward from the Ohio Valley. The state built the Michigan Road in the 1830s between Madison and Michigan City by way of Indianapolis. Privatized after the Civil War as a toll road, this later became State Road 29 and then U.S. Highway 421.[20]

The other important route was the National Road. Like the Michigan Road and many others, it was built in the era of "internal improvements"—publicly financed roads and canals (and even some railroads) intended to open up the interiors of the various states. The federally financed National Road was the most ambitious of all. Proposed in the first decade of the nineteenth century to connect Cumberland, Maryland, with the Ohio River at Wheeling, Virginia (West Virginia after 1863), the road was begun in 1811 and reached the river in 1817. It was built to strict specifications, paved with stone that gave a smooth ride free of dust and mud. An immediate success, it spurred commerce and a market economy previously held back by lack of good transportation. Also called the National Trail and the Cumberland Road, it charged tolls that supported regular maintenance. The National Road paused for some time at the Ohio River, but by the late 1830s it had been extended across Ohio and Indiana to its terminus at Vandalia, Illinois. The road passed through Indianapolis on Washington Street and in the twentieth century became U.S. Route 40, part of the new national highway system.

The Internal Improvements Movement

Young western states needed good transportation, but investment capital was scarce, keeping private interests from building all the toll roads—"turnpikes"—the region needed. But could government step in where private parties did not? Public initiative (could it be called infrastructure or even stimulus spending?) would spread the costs of "internal improvements" across a state's population, with benefits accruing to everyone. Indeed, the creation of the state of Indiana included a provision that 5 percent of the proceeds from federal land sales be used for roads and canals, with three of those percentage points placed under the state legislature's control.[21] This gift financed the Michigan Road, other roads and turnpikes, improvement of navigation on the Wabash River, and partial construction of the Wabash and Erie Canal. Influenced by examples such as the Erie Canal and by increasing talk of the "rail road," Indiana bought into internal improvements in a way that quickly proved much too big. The state's colorfully named "Mammoth Internal Improvement" program of 1836 envisioned eight projects using the "3 percent fund" to build roads, canals, railroads, and river improvements, but the whole plan quickly went sour. A historian writing in 1870 noted acerbically that "it was good while it lasted," but it nearly sank Indiana financially. Only 22 percent of the proposed improvements were completed, but they ate up half of the available funds, a situation aggravated by the Panic of 1837: "The whole cost was money thrown in the water."[22]

Well, not entirely. Some uncompleted projects were finished under private ownership, and by various bond issues and other means Indiana had by 1870 worked its way out from under the debt load. The most expensive and least successful project was the Central Canal, intended to connect the Wabash and Erie Canal with Evansville by way of Indianapolis. After close to a million dollars had been spent, only nine miles of canal were operating between Broad Ripple and Indianapolis. In an example of lemons being made into lemonade, the much-modified canal today is a major recreational asset for the city.[23]

The Canal Era

Despite such sorry tales, the brief ascendancy of the canal had a positive effect on the economies of the midwestern states. Canals bridged the developmental gap between lake/river/road and railroad transportation, a period of only about twenty-five years. If natural waterways were too shallow, rocky, curvy, or otherwise unsuitable for navigation, or if they did not go where they were needed, and if roads were too few or too poor to be of much use, then artificial waterways could open the interior Midwest

The Commercial dream of early Indpls. before Rail roads ————— What might have been but Rail Roads awoke the dreamers.

Figure 1.7 Safer and more predictable journeys could be made on artificial waterways—canals. Despite some false starts, Indiana did have by the mid-1800s a functioning canal system that materially boosted the state's economy. However, Indianapolis was not to benefit from this travel mode. The caption reads, "Commercial dream of early Indpls. before Railroads, what might have been but Rail Roads awoke the dreamers."

Indiana Historical Society, Bass Photo Co. Collection

Figure 1.8 Likely dating from the 1950s, this southward-looking view shows the Central Canal in a sorry state, a condition which fortunately has been corrected, giving Indianapolis a fine recreational waterway. On the right is the former Big Four Railroad's original line to Chicago, which by this time was only an industrial spur. The dome of the 1888 state capitol rises in the background.

Indiana Historical Society, Bass Photo Co. Collection

Figure 1.9 In early 1843 the Madison & Indianapolis Rail Road took over the unfinished rail route that the state had begun as a link between Indianapolis and the Ohio River. At this time the line had not quite reached Columbus, and Indianapolis was still four years and many miles away, but the company wanted to assure the traveling and shipping public that it was a going enterprise offering affordable and safe service.

Indiana Historical Society

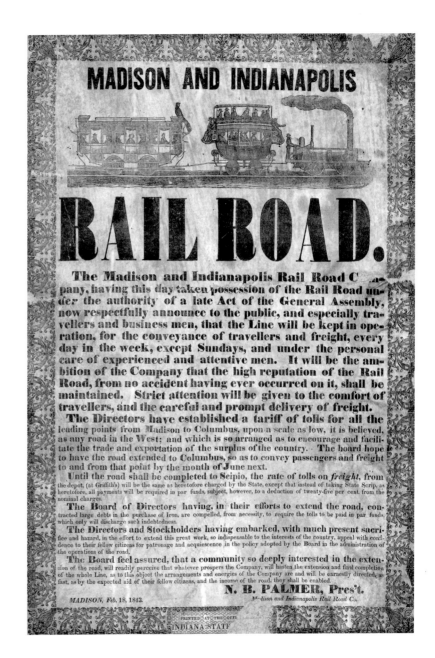

to trade and commerce. A canal's principal disadvantages—its slow pace; its susceptibility to delay due to flooding, low water, siltation, or structural failure; and its suspension of service in the winter—were more than outweighed by its high carrying capacity. By one account, the maximum load for a horse-drawn wagon was one ton, while a one-horse canal boat could carry up to fifty tons,[24] an enormous increase in the amount of cargo that could be moved by the expenditure of a given amount of energy. Particularly for shipments of bulk commodities such as grain, sand, coal, or gravel, where regularity of delivery rather than speed was important, the canal proved to be the right technology at the right time. Passengers, too, often preferred canal packet boats to buggies or stagecoaches.

The American canal system, most of which was built in something of a fevered rush over about a forty-year period ending in the mid-1850s, was almost all located east of the Mississippi River, with the greatest mileage in New York, Pennsylvania, Ohio, Indiana, and Illinois. New England and the mid-Atlantic states had some canals, but the southern states had hardly any. West of the Mississippi, "canal fever" never took hold to any extent, not only because of lack of water and the often severe topography, but also because major settlement there occurred after the railroad had proved its superiority over artificial waterways.

The Canal Era coincided with the dawn of the Railroad Era, and it quickly became a lopsided contest between the two modes. Railroads operated year-round, had greater carrying capacity, required fewer operators for a given amount of cargo, were more comfortable for passengers, could go places canals could not, and were much faster than the four miles an hour that most canal boats achieved. However, in the final accounting canals proved to be not only useful but also economically successful. They generally paid off their first costs and also their ongoing operating costs, and the effect they had on stimulating economic development more than justified those expenses.

Largely forgotten today except by historians and waterway enthusiasts, the nation's canals played a brief but important role in the growth of trade and commerce and helped set the stage for the next revolution in transportation technology. In Indiana during the fourth decade of the nineteenth century, a new form of land transportation began creeping toward the Hoosier capital, with significant implications for how that city would develop over succeeding decades.

NOTES

1. Doris Kearns Goodwin, *Team of Rivals* (New York City: Simon & Schuster, 2006), 28–29.

2. Lorna Hainesworth, "Historic National Road: An All American Road," *Maryland Historic National Road* website, 2011, p. 10. Available at http://marylandnationaroad.org/wp-content/themes/mnra/pdfs/Historic-National-Road.pdf.

3. During an evaluation of the system some Ohio townships were drawn five miles on a side and contained twenty-five one-mile-square sections, but the thirty-six-square-mile section became the standard.

4. The old expression "40 acres and a mule" referred to what was considered the standard for a rural family's farm parcel—that is, the minimum land and motive power required for a typical farm family to raise enough crops to survive.

5. Joseph S. Mendinghall, *The Beginning Point of the First Public Land Survey*, National Park Service, National Register of Historic Places Inventory–Nomination Form, 1974.

6. Richard Sisson, Christian Zacher, and Andrew Cayton, eds., *The American Midwest* (Bloomington: Indiana University Press, 2007), 307.

7. David J. Bodenhamer and Robert G. Barrows, eds., *The Encyclopedia of Indianapolis* (Bloomington: Indiana University Press, 1994), 1007–8, 1165.

8. J. B. Jackson, *Landscapes* (Amherst: University of Massachusetts Press, 1970), 4.

9. James E. Vance Jr., "The American Urban Geography," in *Cities: The Forces That Shape Them*, ed. Lisa Taylor (New York: Cooper-Hewitt Museum, 1982), 23.

10. Jackson, 4.

11. Witold Rybczynski, *A Clearing in the Distance* (New York: Scribner, 2003), 329.

12. Bodenhamer and Barrows, 1007–8.

13. *Plat of the Town of Indianapolis*, Indiana State Library.

14. George Pogue was an early settler and blacksmith who lived in a cabin "built on the south-east bank of the creek that took its name from him, at the east end of the Donation." In 1821 Pogue, then about fifty years old, disappeared while seeking some horses he believed had been stolen by a group of Delaware Indians. John H. B. Nowland, *Early Reminiscences of Indianapolis* (Indianapolis: Sentinel Book and Job Printing House, 1870), 20–21.

15. Bodenhamer and Barrows, 1007–8.

16. Frederic L. Paxson, "The Railroads of the 'Old Northwest' before the Civil War," *Transactions of the Wisconsin Academy of Sciences, Arts, and Letters* 17, part 1 (October 1912): n.p.

See the website of the Catskill Archive, http://www.catskillarchive.com/rrextra/abonw.Html, to find this intriguing work. It contains summary railroad histories and early mileage totals for the five states of the former Northwest Territory, namely Ohio, Indiana, Illinois, Michigan, and Wisconsin.

17. Robert G. Barrows and Leigh Darbee, "The Urban Frontier in Pioneer Indiana," *Indiana Magazine of History* 105, no. 3 (September 2009): 265–6.

18. Bodenhamer and Barrows, 189, 1202.

19. Ibid., 190.

20. Ibid., 1002.

21. Daniel Wait Howe, "A Descriptive Catalogue of the Official Publications of the Territory and State of Indiana from 1800 to 1890," *Indiana Historical Society Publications* 2, no. 5 (Indianapolis: Bowen-Merrill Co., 1886), 190–3.

22. W. R. Holloway, *Indianapolis: A Historical and Statistical Sketch of the Railroad City* (Indianapolis: Indianapolis Journal Print, 1870), 51.

23. Bodenhamer and Barrows, 190.

24. Thomas Crump, *The Age of Steam* (London: Constable & Robinson, 2007), 12.

2

THE RAILROAD ARRIVES:
A NEW TRAVEL TECHNOLOGY

TECHNOLOGICAL CHANGE COMES so quickly today that each new advance—in flight, medicine, automobile design, computers, any of a thousand things—often elicits little response. We are conditioned to expect the Next Big Thing and, when it arrives, we are already waiting for Version 2.0. So it may be difficult to imagine the effect the railroad had on Americans in the era before the Civil War. The low friction and high load-carrying capacity of a flanged wheel on a rail was known as early as medieval times, but it took until the early nineteenth century for this technology to be proven, in England, and to take hold as something truly new. Once this happened, and once it caught the attention of the young United States, the "rail road" gained a firm grip on the American imagination.

Excitement about the railroad was a natural corollary of America's belief in "Progress." By the time the railroad appeared on the scene, the citizens of the young nation were already imbued with a sense of destiny. The national attitude was that economic growth and prosperity, linked inextricably to individual rights, personal freedom, and self-determination, were a birthright. What better means of bringing all of that to fruition than this new means of transportation? The words of observers of the period can give us a sense of their excitement, hope for the future, and, not least, expectation of economic benefit from the railroad. One example of florid praise of the railroad was published in 1850 when the first railroad reached Columbus, Ohio:

> Thus, for the first time, was opened to the people of this region a system of transit, destined immediately to supplant, and almost render obsolete all other modes of conveyance. It is difficult to realize how *sudden* and *complete* is to be the revolution, by entire communities, in their *modes* for the transaction of business, or the pursuit of pleasure. But such is the elasticity of the American mind, and such the indomitable proclivity of the American character, that we shall very soon become familiarized to this transition—and the only wonder will be that any system less prompt and energetic was ever tolerated for a day![1]

Train travel soon became commonplace, and any community of even modest size was convinced that obtaining rail service was nothing less than a rite of passage. This passion came to be known as "railroad fever" and would not subside until the early twentieth century, with the nation's railroad mileage peaking at the time of World War I. Suggesting some sort of disease, the term was often used derisively to describe the many unwise, undercapitalized, foolish, and fantastic railroad-building schemes that flourished like mushrooms after a rain. The American business landscape is littered with the carcasses of such enterprises, many of which seemed compelled to include "& Pacific" in their corporate names.

Indiana was not immune to the fever. Among its earliest railroads were two proposed in the disastrous Mammoth Internal Improvement Act of 1836, one to connect Madison with Indianapolis, and the other to reach southeast from the capital toward Cincinnati. The state failed to complete them, although it did get a start on the rail line from the Ohio River at Madison. Most of the unfinished state improvements were turned over to private investors, who eventually saw to it that both rail routes did get built. Undoubtedly the going was rough for many early railroads, as historian W. R. Holloway noted: "The railroad fever was taken early in Indiana, but its energy was expended idly because applied prematurely. If the lines at first proposed could have been built they would have languished, and possibly have died, before the development of the country could have supplied them with profitable business."[2] He went on to note that by 1830 six rail lines had been proposed between Indianapolis and the southern part of the state and that all were abandoned except for the Madison line, which the state managed to get up and out of the Ohio River valley and on to Vernon by 1841. There it would stay until the privately built Madison & Indianapolis (M&I) finally took it over and made it the first railroad to enter the capital city.

Even with accurate projections of traffic and revenues, building something as large and capital-intensive as a railroad was full of risk. As Frederic Paxson stated, "In a large proportion of cases railway construction began at points already well established in trade or industry; and advanced to the unknown from the known"[3]—that is, to undeveloped territory lacking people and commerce to keep a railroad economically viable. It often was not the railroad promoter who took the greatest financial risk, since he seldom had much of his own funds in the enterprise. It was instead the purchasers of railroad stocks and bonds—small businesses, cities and villages, farmers, state governments, and foreign investors—who stood to lose the most.

However, railroad fever did not result only in crackpot schemes and pie-in-the-sky projections of success. It was a period when a varied cast of characters—civic boosters, financiers, speculators, engineers, hardheaded businessmen, visionaries—frequently in fits and starts, put in place the core of the national railroad network that still serves us today. Even failed railroad promotions often had future benefits: after nascent railroad schemes collapsed due to mismanagement, fraud, or other causes, they often left assets such as rights-of-way, roadbeds, and bridge abutments available at bargain prices to be picked up by other, more competent companies. The Madison & Indianapolis was only the first of many such examples in Indiana.

As rail lines began operating, they had positive economic effects on the communities they served, and books and articles began to document this trend. One boosterish example was a notice in an early national railroad guide ponderously titled *American Railway Guide, and Pocket Companion, for the United States; Containing Correct Tables for Time of Starting from All Stations, Distances, Fares, Etc. on All the Railway Lines in the United States; Together with a Complete Railway Map.* The May 1852 edition of 27,200 copies, priced at 12.5 cents each, contained the following:

> Benefit of Railroads.—In 1834 Massachusetts commenced making railroads. In 1840 she had finished, and had in operation, 167 miles, and about 650 miles in process of construction. On 1st Jan., 1840, the returned value of all the property in the state was $299,878,329. At the same period, in 1851, 1142 miles of railroad had been built, at a cost of $51,873,815, and the value of property was shown to have increased in the eleven past years to $666,252,581, being an advance of 367 millions [sic] dollars, or more than double what it was in 1840. This increased value is nearly equal to $52,500 to each square mile of her territory, and the aggregate average value of every citizen of that old State has doubled, while the rate of taxation has been reduced more than one-half. Such facts as the above are more convincing than the most elaborate arguments, and ought to be well considered of by all States.[4]

The clear implication was that the railroads of Massachusetts had spurred all of the state's increase in wealth. Even their most ardent supporters might not give railroads this much credit, but they did become a major economic development tool, enabling the United States to emerge in the late nineteenth and early twentieth centuries as a commercial and industrial powerhouse. As with any new technology, there were opponents and doubters who were not at all certain that the railroad was a good thing. There were few instances where opposition blocked a proposed rail route, but contrary voices must have been loud enough to prompt some early railroad boosters to go to great lengths to make their case. Here is one example, under the title "The Value and Importance of Railroads":

> We have heard of a farmer in the Tenth Legion of Virginia, who is an unbeliever in the benefit of railroads, and opposed to his county's giving any encouragement to the making of one through it. As there may be "more of the same sort" in that region of the Ancient Dominion, we insert for their edification, if they "ever read the papers," the subjoined forcible article from the Philadelphia *Inquirer*, and which we understand is from the practical pen of the Hon. Joel B. Sutherland, of Pennsylvania.
>
> *From the Philadelphia Inquirer.* The railroad interest is sadly depressed at the present time. We are sorry, moreover, to see a disposition in some quarters still further to depreciate this invaluable species of property. The railroads are among the essentials of the age, No great country can do without them. They facilitate trade and travel, increase the value of land, and open up to the hardy pioneer new homes and fresh sources of independence and wealth. What, indeed, would Philadelphia, New York, Boston, and Baltimore be without railroads? What would be the condition of the mighty West at this time but for these great highways, these links of steel which bind the Union together in a common brotherhood?[5]

The author of the *Inquirer* article gave more than twenty additional reasons to support railroads, among them that without rail transport the trade and commerce of the nation would grind to a halt within a week; he also argued that carrying the mail by rail would not allow robbers to "bear away the letters." The "sadly depressed" state of the "railroad interest" at the time of writing was due to the virulent Panic of 1857, an economic collapse that, like others that would follow, slowed but did not halt railroad development.

In the end, of course, railroad boosters won the argument. In the Midwest the Railroad Era dawned less like the rising sun than like a supernova, with promoters proposing railroad lines from everywhere to everywhere. "Midwest" is an imprecise term, the definition of which varies, but any fair description of the region must include its beating heart: Ohio, Indiana, and Illinois, where a great deal of pre–Civil War railroad construction took place. Despite all the vicissitudes that came with developing a new technology that had to be flung across hundreds of miles of territory, and that then had somehow to sustain itself until it achieved a paying traffic base, a working national railroad network had been put in place, piece by piece and mile by mile, between the early 1850s and the late 1890s.

The Fruits of "Railroad Fever"

What the various railroad companies accomplished in this short period of time, almost entirely by human and animal power, with a good dose of black powder when needed, was remarkable. By the early 1850s, the Baltimore & Ohio Railroad, after an exhausting quarter-century push westward through some of the most forbidding Appalachian terrain, found itself on the east bank of the Ohio River at Wheeling, Virginia. Yet within four years, the B&O, through connections with affiliated midwestern lines, could offer through service to the Mississippi River at St. Louis. These accomplishments were saluted publicly in the form of the Great Railway Celebrations of 1857, the self-congratulatory event sponsored by the B&O and documented in William Prescott Smith's *The Book of the Great Railway Celebrations of 1857*, which was published the following year.

A little to the north, the Pennsylvania Railroad in 1854 had opened its all-rail route between Philadelphia and Pittsburgh, replacing the much-maligned rail-and-canal system that had served for some twenty years. Yet by the time of the B&O's celebrations, the "Pennsy" offered through service to Chicago. Its great rival, the New York Central Railroad, had been stitched together in 1853 from nearly a dozen smaller roads in upstate New York, but by 1857 it, too, connected New York City and Chicago with a main line through central New York, northwestern Pennsylvania, and the northern counties of Ohio and Indiana. This it had achieved through connections with several railroads that would become the Lake Shore & Michigan Southern Railroad. By the time of the Civil War, the Hoosier State was fifth among the states in railroad route mileage, after New York, Ohio, Illinois, and Pennsylvania. At this time all five states were served by railroad "trunk" lines connecting the country's major commercial centers. These railroads were the "roots of the routes" to the ultimate goal, the West Coast.

Indiana participated enthusiastically in what could only be called a frenzy of railroad building in the fourteen years between the opening of its first railroad, the Madison & Indianapolis, and the start of the Civil War. From the M&I's 86 miles in 1847, the

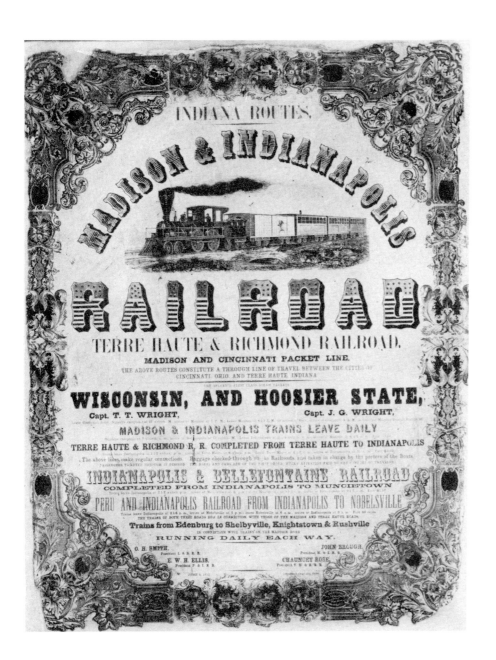

Figure 2.1 Following the Madison & Indianapolis's 1847 arrival in Indianapolis, other rail routes soon reached the city. This broadside advertised all the places one could travel from stations on the M&I by both rail and water. "Muncietown," for example, could be visited via the Indianapolis & Bellefontaine Railroad, which became the Big Four's Cleveland line and is still an important freight route today.

1854 AIR LINE RAIL ROAD. 1854

WESTERN PASSENGERS!
TAKE NOTICE,

FROM ALBANY,

To Indianapolis, Ind. Lafayette, Ind. Terra Haute, Ind. Madison, Ind.
AND LOUISVILLE, KY.
BY THE
NEW YORK CENTRAL R. R. to Buffalo, **LAKE SHORE R. R.** to Cleveland
AND

CLEVELAND & BELLEFONTAINE & INDIANAPOLIS

RAIL ROAD.

3 EXPRESS TRAINS LEAVE ALBANY DAILY, New Road,
[SUNDAYS EXCEPTED.]

7.30 A. M. & 12.00 M. EXPRESS TRAINS,

Connect at Buffalo with the 10.30 P. M. train on the Lake Shore Rail Road, and at Cleveland with the Express trains on the Cleveland & Bellefontaine & Indianapolis R. R. for Bellefontaine, Urbana, Springfield and Dayton. Passengers for Dayton will find this the Quickest Route, arriving at Dayton at 4 P. M. This train arrives at Indianapolis at 9 P. M., and trains leave Indianapolis for Madison, Terra Haute, Lafayette Ind. Louisville, Ky. at 6. AM.—arriving at Louisville in time to take the Steamers for St. Louis and New Orleans the same afternoon.

11.00 P. M. EXPRESS TRAIN,

Connects at Buffalo with the 10.45 A. M. train on the Lake Shore R. R. and at Cleveland with the 8.30 P. M. Express train on the Cleveland & Bellefontaine & Indianapolis R. R. direct for Dayton, Bellefontaine, Indianapolis, Madison, Terra Haute, Lafayette, Ind., and Louisville, Ky.—arriving at Indianapolis at 10.30 A. M. and Louisville same afternoon.

☞ Passengers by taking this route for Louisville, Ky. St. Louis, or any places on the Ohio and Mississippi Rivers, at or below Madison, Ind. arrive at Madison, or Louisville, Ky. about the same time the Steamers leave Cincinnati. FARE ABOUT THE SAME.

In Advance of any other Route.

FARE, FIRST CLASS.

From Albany to Louisville, Ky. $18.00	From Albany to Dayton, Ohio.	$14.75
" Lafayette, Ind. 18.00	" Sidney, "	14.10
" Madison, Ind. 18.00	" Bellefontaine, "	13.50
" Indianapolis, Id. 16.00	" Marion, "	12.50
" Terra Haute, Id. 18.00	2d. Class to Indianapolis,	10.00

Baggage Checked from Albany to Buffalo, & thence to Bellefontaine & Indianapolis,
From there to all other Points named Above.

☞ Procure Tickets at the New York Central R. R. Office, in Albany.

Merchants wishing to ship Goods, can make contracts in New York, Boston, Albany or Troy, with the General Freight Agt. of the R. R. Companies, or Erie Canal Lines, to whom through Freight Tariffs will be sent. Goods addressed to care of L. M. HUBBY, Agent C. C. & C. R. R. Cleveland, will be forwarded with despatch.

J. NOTTINGHAM, Sup't.

For information relative to the above Routes apply to

Albany, March, 1854.   H. O. PAGE, Agt. N. Y. C. R. R. Depot.

Figure 2.2 Westward-bound migrant traffic was important in the second half of the nineteenth century. By the mid-1850s the East and the Midwest were linked by several railroads that crossed Indiana, though not always through Indianapolis. The "Air Line Railroad" was not an actual railroad; this term indicated a straight and direct route. All of the lines noted in this poster later became part of the Big Four and then the New York Central. Those easterners had not yet learned how to spell "Terre Haute."

Indiana Historical Society

state's railroad mileage grew to 228 by 1850 and then exploded to 2,163 by 1860. The war slowed railroad development, but Indiana added another 1,014 miles of line between 1860 and 1870. The mileage peak came between 1910 and 1920, when the state was served by some 7,420 route miles of railroad, a figure that had declined to a little less than 6,600 by 1960.[6] Today there are just under 4,500 miles of railroad lines in Indiana.[7]

The five leading states in railroad mileage in the pre–Civil War era had the following totals as of 1855: New York, 2,685 miles; Ohio, 2,453; Illinois, 1,884; Pennsylvania, 1,581; and Indiana, 1,406. Massachusetts was next, with 1,220 miles, and the rest of the states ranged well behind these six, claiming between 22 and 986 miles.[8]

By 1870, the Civil War's negative effect on railroad building had faded away: national rail mileage in 1860 was 30,626; in 1865, 35,085, and in 1870, 52,922.[9] Mileage in the South had increased considerably, but the greatest density of rail lines remained in southern New England, eastern Pennsylvania, and Ohio, Indiana, and Illinois. The Union Pacific/Central Pacific transcontinental railroad was in service, and west of the Mississippi numerous railroads were beginning to stretch across Minnesota, Iowa, Missouri, and Kansas.

Between 1870 and 1890 much of the rest of the nation's railroad network was put in place, with over 70,000 miles of road built just between 1880 and 1890. In 1890 the rail routes of the United States totaled 163,597 miles. Construction continued into the new century, reaching a peak of 254,037 miles of line in 1916. By 1950 the total was down to 223,427 miles and by 1960 to 217,552. Today the country is served by around 140,000 miles of line, not far above half the total for 1916 but vastly more efficient and with far greater carrying capacity than a century ago.

Indiana filled out its railroad map along with the other states, multiplying its 1,406 miles in 1855 to the 7,400 or so that it could claim around 1916. By 1920, however, the state had dropped to thirteenth in mileage but remained, then as today, the locus of major east–west trunk line railroad routes.

INDIANAPOLIS, THE "CROSSROADS OF AMERICA"

Population figures for Indianapolis in the first half of the nineteenth century support the conclusion that lack of good land and water transportation was a drag on growth. Even though it was the state's capital, Indianapolis in 1830 had a population of no more than 1,900, while the river cities of Cincinnati and Louisville had roughly 25,000 and 10,000 citizens respectively.[10] Indianapolis had grown from roughly 600 citizens five years earlier but clearly was behind communities with better transportation. The National Road, which traversed Indianapolis along the line of Washington Street, spurred the city's population growth to nearly 2,700 by 1840. However, by the next census that figure was just over 8,000; it would reach nearly 19,000 by 1860, and just over 48,000 by 1870, nearly an eighteenfold increase over the figure for 1840. Clearly something had happened to cause this growth. Indeed, historians have frequently divided the story of Indianapolis into periods before and after October 1, 1847, when the Madison & Indianapolis Railroad connected the capital city with the Ohio River. It would be hard to dispute that this rail line and others soon to follow were the primary influence upon the city's surge in population by 1850. Twenty years later, the Indianapolis railroad

Baltimore & Ohio
RAILROAD,
CONNECTING
ALL PARTS OF THE EAST
WITH
ALL PARTS OF THE WEST,
AND
The Shortest Route
BETWEEN
NEW YORK, PHILADELPHIA, BALTIMORE & WASHINGTON,
AND
COLUMBUS, CINCINNATI, LOUISVILLE, DAYTON, INDIANAPOLIS, ST. LOUIS, CAIRO, MEMPHIS and NEW ORLEANS.

This Great Railroad is located nearly upon the line formerly traveled by the NATIONAL ROAD, running between the Cities of *WASHINGTON* and *BALTIMORE* and the Commercial Cities of the OHIO AND MISSISSIPPI VALLEYS.

Through Tickets
FOR THE WESTERN CITIES, AND
BAGGAGE CHECKS,
By the Baltimore and Ohio Railroad and its various Connecting Lines, may be had at
NEW YORK, PHILADELPHIA, BALTIMORE & WASHINGTON.

FREIGHT OF ALL KINDS,
In any quantity, will be carried by Through Receipt, in the Quickest Time, and at the Lowest Rates.

For Particulars, see Newspaper Advertisements and Handbills.

Figure 2.3 (*Left*) By the time of the Great Railway Celebrations of 1857, Indianapolis was among the key "western" cities served by the Baltimore & Ohio Railroad, although at this time only by means of connecting carriers. The note about the railroad following "nearly upon" the route of the National Road probably was meant to reassure train riders that they would be traveling a well-known direct route and would not be forced to pass through wild and dangerous places.

Author's collection

Figure 2.4 (*Facing*) This two-page ad from the B&O's 1858 celebratory book focused on generating traffic from Ohio, but it featured Indianapolis as one of the destinations. Compared to ads from just a few years earlier, this one was much more westward-oriented, looking beyond Indiana to places such as Kansas, Nebraska, and New Orleans. The nation's relentless march to the far West was under way.

Author's collection

GREAT NATIONAL ROUTE

East and West.

CENTRAL OHIO

RAILROAD,

A Short and Direct Route

BETWEEN

New York, Boston, Philadelphia,

BALTIMORE, WASHINGTON,

And All Eastern Cities,

AND

COLUMBUS,

CINCINNATI, LOUISVILLE, DAYTON,

INDIANAPOLIS, ST. LOUIS,

CAIRO, KANSAS, NEBRASKA and

NEW ORLEANS,

AND ALL POINTS SOUTH AND WEST.

This Road connects at BELLAIRE, opposite Benwood, (4 miles below Wheeling,) with the

BALTIMORE AND OHIO,

AND THE

WHEELING & PITTSBURG RAILROADS,

For All Points East.

☞At ZANESVILLE, with the

CINCINNATI, WILMINGTON AND ZANESVILLE RAILROAD,

For Lancaster, Circleville, Washington, &c.

☞At NEWARK, with the

Sandusky, Mansfield and Newark R. R.

FOR

Mt. Vernon, Mansfield, Sandusky, Toledo, Detroit, Chicago, &c.

☞At COLUMBUS, with

THE LITTLE MIAMI

AND

COLUMBUS, PIQUA AND INDIANA RAILROADS,

For Indianapolis, Cincinnati, St. Louis, Cairo and

☞ ALL POINTS SOUTH AND WEST. ☜

Passengers taking the EXPRESS TRAIN will have

NO CHANGE OF CARS BETWEEN WHEELING & CINCINNATI

Ask for Tickets via WHEELING (or BELLAIRE) and COLUMBUS.

Great Stock and Freight Route.

Shippers will find it to their interest to take this route. Through Bills of Lading given to all Eastern Cities, at as low rates as any other Railroad route, and all Freight transported with

REGULARITY & DISPATCH.

H. J. JEWETT, Pres't,
Zanesville, Ohio.

D. S. GRAY,   **JNO. W. BROWN,**
GEN'L FREIGHT AGENT,   GEN'L TICKET AGENT,
Columbus, Ohio.   *Columbus, Ohio.*

map showed eleven different lines serving the city; by that time, the population had increased sixfold.

The arrival of the M&I was greeted with the same breathless enthusiasm that the "iron horse" inspired elsewhere. Typical was this commentary in the *Indiana State Journal* of November 2, 1847. The passage of a month and a day had not cooled the editor's ardor for the new railroad: "Indianapolis has changed. Friday, October 1st, 1847, was an era in our history. On that day we were linked with commerce. From the beginning of the world until that day, the rattling of the cars and the whistling of the locomotive were unknown sounds, but from then until the end of civilization, perhaps to the end of time, these sounds will never die away."

So Indianapolis did get itself a railroad—in fact, quite a few of them, enough to inspire the city to dub itself "the Crossroads of America." By the early 1850s it was well on its way to being tied into the growing national railroad network, a major stop along the way from eastern cities such as New York, Philadelphia, Baltimore, and Washington to western gateways such as Chicago and St. Louis.

That first railroad to reach the Hoosier capital was like other pioneer midwestern roads: it connected an established water route with the state's interior. The Madison & Indianapolis, eighty-six miles in length by way of Columbus, entered Indianapolis from the south and has long been known for its steep grade out of the Ohio River valley at Madison and for the distinctive ten-driving-wheel steam locomotive that resides today in the Children's Museum in Indianapolis. The M&I eventually became part of a railroad serving Louisville, Kentucky, and was later absorbed into the mighty Pennsylvania Railroad.[11] Then, over the next seventy-one years, like spokes being added one by one to the hub of a wheel, new lines filled out the railroad map of Indianapolis so that by 1918 the city's rail network was complete. Much of this railroad building occurred between the 1850s and the 1880s. By 1870, eleven rail routes were in place, and by 1889 the number was up to fourteen. The final two lines opened in 1906 and 1918.

The Railroads of the "Railroad City"

The story of American railroads in the second half of the nineteenth century was one of change, evolution, and absorption into the major systems that dominated the industry through most of the twentieth century. Five of these trunk carriers would, in time, control all but one of the rail routes of Indianapolis: the Baltimore & Ohio Railroad, the Illinois Central Railroad, the New York Central Railroad, the Nickel Plate Road, and the Pennsylvania Railroad. One more, not a major carrier like the others but homegrown and fondly remembered, was the Monon, officially the Chicago, Indianapolis & Louisville Railway. One by one, over some seven decades, the predecessors of these companies had built the tracks, freight terminals, passenger depots, and other facilities that enabled Indianapolis to call itself not only a crossroads but also, by 1870, the "Railroad City."

To a degree seen in few other large cities, the railroads of Indianapolis converged on a single point, a corridor some three blocks south of Monument Circle at the edge of the city's commercial core. This affected the urban form and character of the city in ways that are still evident today. The sixteen railroad

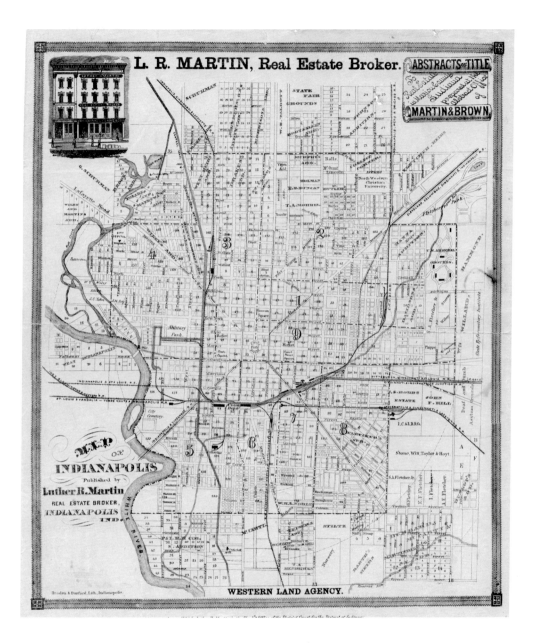

Figure 2.5 The original Mile Square is visible on this 1870 map of Indianapolis, with numerous extensions of its original street grid and diagonal avenues. Eleven railroad routes are shown, heading to all points of the compass, and the wisdom of locating Union Depot along Louisiana Street is readily apparent. The city's railroads had abandoned their separate depots by this time, though they often kept freight facilities at or near their former depot sites.

Indiana Historical Society, G4894

29

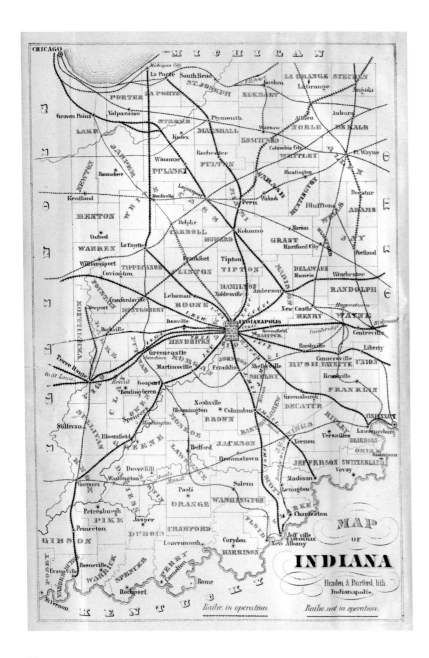

Figure 2.6 Holloway's 1870 history of Indianapolis showed how quickly the Hoosier capital had become the nexus of Indiana railroad routes. Although this map suggests that all lines to and through the city were equally important, in fact the east–west routes carried the heaviest traffic. Chicago, destined to be the nation's rail capital, was at this time reached only by an indirect routing.

Indiana Historical Society

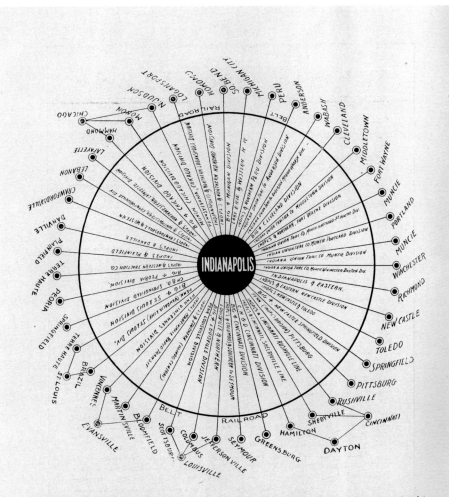

MAP Showing Indianapolis as a Steam Railroad and Interurban Center. At this date 43 Independent Lines enter Our City, 18 Steam and 25 Interurban. 495 passenger trains enter our Union Stations daily. A Belt Railroad surrounds the city, expediting shipments and furnishing factory sites. One-fourth of the population of the United States is within a radius of three hundred miles of Indianapolis.

Figure 2.7 By 1907, when this compass-like device was published, fifteen of the sixteen steam railroad routes that would serve Indianapolis were in place. This was a promotional or "booster" piece that showed the many places accessible by rail from the Hoosier capital, as well as the Belt Railroad that tied all the city's railroads together. It also showed the various interurban routes that radiated from Indianapolis.

Indiana Historical Society

Table 2.1 The completion dates of the 16 rail routes that served Indianapolis from the mid-nineteenth century into the late twentieth century fall into three time periods: pre–Civil War routes, 1847 to 1854; post–Civil War routes, 1869 to 1883; and early-twentieth-century routes. In this table, the six different railroads in the Final Name/System column predate the late-twentieth-century consolidations of major eastern railroads into Conrail, Norfolk Southern, and CSX Transportation.

Pre–Civil War Routes

Year	Original Name	Final Name/System	Destination Cities
1847	Madison & Indianapolis	Pennsylvania	Madison, Louisville
1850	Indianapolis & Bellefontaine	New York Central	Muncie, Cleveland
1852	Lafayette & Indianapolis	New York Central	Lafayette, Chicago
1852	Terre Haute & Richmond	Pennsylvania	Terre Haute, St. Louis
1853	Indianapolis & Cincinnati	New York Central	Shelbyville, Cincinnati
1853	Indiana Central	Pennsylvania	Richmond, Pittsburgh
1854	Peru & Indianapolis	Norfolk & Western	Peru, Michigan City

Post–Civil War Routes

Year	Original Name	Final Name/System	Destination Cities
1869	Indianapolis & Vincennes	Pennsylvania	Gosport, Vincennes
1869	Cincinnati & Indianapolis Junction	Baltimore & Ohio	Connersville, Cincinnati
1869	Indpls Crawfordsville & Danville	New York Central	Crawfordsville, Peoria
1870	Indianapolis & St. Louis	New York Central	Terre Haute, St. Louis
1880	Indpls, Decatur & Springfield	Baltimore & Ohio	Roachdale, Springfield (IL)
1882	Indiana, Bloomington & Western	New York Central	New Castle, Springfield (OH)
1883	Louisville, New Albany & Chicago	Monon	Frankfort, Chicago

Early-Twentieth-Century Routes

Year	Original Name	Final Name/System	Destination Cities
1906	Indianapolis Southern	Illinois Central	Bloomington, Effingham (IL)
1918	Indianapolis & Frankfort	Pennsylvania	Logansport, Chicago

routes that served Indianapolis are listed in table 2.1, which shows the dates they were completed between their intended terminal cities, their original names, the five larger systems into which all but the Monon were absorbed, and other Indiana cities they served.

New York Central Railroad

The New York Central Railroad had the most Indianapolis routes. Between 1850 and 1882, predecessors built six lines that entered the city from the north, northeast, southeast, west, and northwest. By 1930, all had been consolidated under the New York Central (NYC) and extended eastward to Cleveland, Columbus, and Cincinnati, Ohio; and westward to St. Louis, Missouri, and Peoria and Chicago, Illinois.

The first NYC predecessor was the Indianapolis & Bellefontaine ("Bell-FOUN-t'n") Railroad (I&B), opened in 1850 between Indianapolis and Union City on the Ohio state line. Through later combinations, this route ran to Cleveland via Bellefontaine and Galion, Ohio; in 1889 it became part of the Cleveland, Cincinnati, Chicago & St. Louis Railway (the "Big Four"), which was leased in 1930 to the New York Central. The I&B route came into Indianapolis from the northeast via Muncie. Today, carrying heavy traffic, it parallels Massachusetts Avenue on the north before traversing several curves to turn west toward Union Station.

In 1852 the Lafayette & Indianapolis Railroad (L&I) opened between its namesake communities. By 1867 it had been absorbed by the Indianapolis, Cincinnati & Lafayette Railroad, which was destined to be an important line between Cincinnati and Chicago. This in turn was absorbed in 1889 by the Big Four and for many years hosted the *James Whitcomb Riley* between Cincinnati and Chicago. The L&I entered Indianapolis from the north along the west side of the city's downtown. This line was later relocated farther west and connected with the Peoria & Eastern Railroad (see below) to turn east toward Union Station. Much of the route between Chicago and Indianapolis has been abandoned, although some segments are operated by short lines.

The Indianapolis & Cincinnati Railroad (I&C) opened in 1853, entering the city from the southeast and turning west along the line of Louisiana Street to Union Station. The I&C subsequently became the Indianapolis, Cincinnati & Lafayette and then part of the Big Four and the New York Central. It no longer forms a through route to Cincinnati, but it serves the former NYC passenger car shops at Beech Grove, Amtrak's principal repair and maintenance facility.

The Indianapolis, Crawfordsville & Danville Railroad opened in 1869 and merged that same year with a western partner, the Danville, Urbana, Bloomington & Pekin Railroad, which had been organized in 1867. The merged property, the Indianapolis, Bloomington & Western Railroad, failed in 1874 and emerged in 1879 as the Indiana, Bloomington & Western Railroad (IB&W). In 1882 this road joined a new route from Indianapolis to Springfield and Columbus, Ohio, all under the IB&W banner. Another receivership in 1886 resulted in two new companies east and west of Indianapolis that were soon merged as the Ohio, Indiana & Western Railroad. Still suffering financial troubles, the property was foreclosed in 1890. The Big Four purchased the eastern portion, and a new company, the Peoria & Eastern Railroad, acquired the western portion and then leased it to the Big Four.

Figure 2.8 This was the face of railroading in Indianapolis until the mid-twentieth century. New York Central Hudson-type locomotive number 5401 wheels train number 3, the *James Whitcomb Riley*, westbound out of Union Station at Kentucky Avenue on November 11, 1949. The train's cars are all sided in fluted stainless steel, part of the Central's postwar Great Steel Fleet, which would soldier on for more than twenty years and into the Amtrak era.

Jay Williams/Big Four Graphics collection

Although it forms a portion of Amtrak's route between Chicago and Indianapolis, most of this railroad has been abandoned. On the east side of the city, it diverged from the main Big Four line (the original I&B) around Massachusetts Avenue and 21st Street at DX Tower. On the west side, the line diverged to the northwest from the Union tracks (see chapter 3) west of the White River and just south of where the Indianapolis Zoo is today.

The year 1870 saw completion of the Indianapolis & St. Louis Railroad. Through a connection at Terre Haute with the St. Louis, Alton & Terre Haute Railroad, this line connected Indianapolis and St. Louis. It was undertaken by the Bellefontaine line and others to compete with a route that included the Terre Haute & Richmond (see the Pennsylvania Railroad, below). The Indianapolis & St. Louis leased the St. Louis, Alton & Terre Haute even before the former's route between Indianapolis and Terre Haute was completed, and then in 1889 it merged with the Cleveland, Columbus, Cincinnati & Indianapolis Railroad (the Bee Line, descended from the Indianapolis & Bellefontaine) to form the Big Four. The Indianapolis & St. Louis headed west from Union Station and crossed Washington Street (U.S. Route 40) just west of Big Eagle Creek. Farther west, Avon Yard (also called Big Four Yard) today remains a major freight facility on

this busy line, although the former Indianapolis & St. Louis has been mostly abandoned west of Terre Haute in favor of the former Pennsylvania Railroad's St. Louis line.

The former Peoria & Eastern (New York Central) Railroad line eastward from Indianapolis was referred to in the earlier discussion of the Indiana, Bloomington & Western Railroad. This portion of the IB&W opened in 1882 to connect Indianapolis with Springfield and Columbus, Ohio. Even though it provided a direct connection between the two capital cities, it was always a secondary line operated as part of the New York Central and then the rickety Penn Central; its traffic and physical condition declined, and most of it was abandoned in the mid-1970s. It ran generally north-northeast through Shirley, New Castle, and Lynn, where it turned more easterly and entered Ohio.

Pennsylvania Railroad

The Pennsylvania Railroad (PRR), which once modestly declared itself "the Standard Railroad of the World," had five different routes to Indianapolis from the north, east, south, southwest, and west; they went to Pittsburgh, Philadelphia, and New York City; Louisville, Kentucky; Vincennes, Indiana; St. Louis, Missouri; and Chicago, Illinois. The component companies had by

Figure 2.9 Although most passenger-car switching was handled by each railroad's motive power, Indianapolis Union Railway locomotives also did work along the Union tracks. In an undated view likely from the early 1950s, IU number 8, a Baldwin product built in 1930, moves cars westward on the Union Station bypass tracks.

Jay Williams/Big Four Graphics collection

Figure 2.10 In 1949 or 1950, Ed Nowak, New York Central System photographer, made this view of the Big Four freight house on East South Street. Though the eye is drawn to the New York Central trucks, the Pacemaker Freight Service boxcars, and the lightning-stripe-adorned cab units, the Indianapolis skyline of days past is of considerable interest, too.

Ed Nowak photo, Jay Williams collection

Figure 2.11 (*Above*) There was a lot of freight traffic into and out of downtown Indianapolis even into the late 1950s and early 1960s. New York Central Lima-built number 8404 is handling a cut of cars along the Big Four's original Chicago line, now bypassed by a new routing and relegated to freight service. The Central Canal is in the foreground.

Ron Stuckey photo, John Fuller collection, courtesy of Jay Williams

Figure 2.12 (*Facing*) On a gloomy midwestern day around 1970, Penn Central's *James Whitcomb Riley* departs Union Station, trailing a Penn Central business car full of Indiana Historical Society members. The massive Indianapolis Power & Light generating plant is at left.

Jay Williams

Figure 2.13 The Pennsylvania Railroad was the New York Central's archrival and was the other dominant carrier in Indianapolis. This undated view, looking west from Virginia Avenue, shows PRR K4s number 923 leaving Union Station with an eastbound train.

Jay Williams/Big Four Graphics collection

1916 become part of the Pittsburgh, Cincinnati, Chicago & St. Louis Railroad (the "Pan Handle"), which in turn became part of the Pennsylvania Railroad by lease in 1921. (The odd moniker "Pan Handle," also rendered as "Panhandle," arose from the fact that this line, on its way from Pittsburgh to Columbus, Ohio, and westward, crossed the narrow northern panhandle of West Virginia.)

The pioneer Madison & Indianapolis began construction in Madison and reached the capital city by way of Columbus, using some roadbed previously built by the state. In 1866 the M&I was merged with the Jeffersonville Railroad and became the Jeffersonville, Madison & Indianapolis; because of its easy access to Louisville, Kentucky, the line through Jeffersonville became the main line, leaving Madison at the end of a branch. The Louisville route survives today as the Louisville & Indiana Railroad, and part of the line from Columbus to Madison became a short line that did daily battle with the nearly 6 percent grade up from the Ohio River valley.

In 1852, five years into the railroad era in Indianapolis, the Terre Haute & Richmond Railroad began service and in the following year connected with the Indiana Central as part of a route to northeastern cities. Construction west of Terre Haute by 1870 linked this line to another serving St. Louis, thereby forming a competitor of the Indianapolis & St. Louis (New York Central) for traffic between the East and the Midwest.

The Indiana Central Railway (IC), opened in 1853, ran seventy-four miles between Indianapolis and Richmond, and extended to the Ohio state line at New Paris; there it connected with a Columbus route that would eventually reach New York City, Philadelphia, and Washington, DC. The IC connected at Indianapolis with the Terre Haute & Richmond Railroad and, through a complicated series of mergers, became part of the Pan Handle's main line between New York, Pittsburgh, and St. Louis. As part of Penn Central and then Conrail after the former's collapse, the old Indiana Central carried heavy traffic, but with a shift to the former Bellefontaine/Big Four line, the Pan Handle between Columbus and Indianapolis was largely abandoned in the early 1980s. The IC followed a straight route into Indianapolis from the east, a little south of Washington Street. A small segment east of the city survived to serve local industries through a connection at the east end of the former PRR's Hawthorne Yard.

The Indianapolis & Vincennes Railroad (I&V) was projected as a through route to the Gulf of Mexico but never got

Figure 2.14 "Foreign" locomotives came through Indianapolis as part of the power pool for the *South Wind*, the Chicago–Florida service that ran on the Pennsylvania Railroad from Chicago to Louisville. The Louisville & Nashville and the Atlantic Coast Line took it from there to Florida. Here the train curves onto PRR's Louisville line around 1967 as it leaves Indianapolis Union Station.

Jay Williams photo

beyond Indiana. Completed quickly between 1867 and 1869 to connect its namesake cities, it fell under Pennsylvania Railroad control in 1871 and served as a branch line. Coal was its primary traffic and still is today; the line is now the Indiana Southern Railroad. When it opened in 1869, the I&V entered Indianapolis from the southwest and today follows that original alignment along the west side of Kentucky Avenue (Indiana Route 67). It no longer extends into the downtown area, but instead turns north to connect with the former Pennsylvania Railroad's St. Louis line.

The Pennsylvania's Indianapolis network was completed by the last rail line built to serve the city, the Indianapolis & Frankfort Railroad (I&F), opened in June of 1918. Forty-one miles long, it enabled the PRR to move southern Indiana coal to the Chicago area without using the Lake Erie & Western Railway trackage rights it had once held between Indianapolis and Kokomo. The I&F diverged from the Pan Handle's St. Louis main line at Ben Davis, west of Indianapolis, and turned north toward Lebanon and Frankfort. It once hosted PRR's Louisville and Florida trains, and a short segment of it between the old Peoria & Eastern junction at Clermont and Ben Davis serves Amtrak's Chicago–Indianapolis–Washington, DC, trains.

Baltimore & Ohio Railroad

The venerable Baltimore & Ohio (B&O) was sixth largest in Indiana, with three cross-state routes and branches totaling 585 route miles. The northernmost of the three was the Chicago line; the southernmost was the St. Louis line; and the central line through Indianapolis extended from Cincinnati to Springfield, Illinois. The Cincinnati & Indianapolis Junction Railroad opened in 1869 and within three years became part of the Cincinnati, Hamilton & Indianapolis Railroad. It and the line west of Indianapolis were merged in 1902 as the Cincinnati, Indianapolis & Western Railroad, which that same year was leased to the Cincinnati, Hamilton & Dayton Railway (CH&D); the B&O acquired the CH&D in 1927.

The B&O west of Indianapolis was organized in 1869 as the Indianapolis, Decatur & Springfield Railroad (ID&S). Partial service began in 1875, and the line reached Indianapolis in 1880. The ID&S went through several corporate changes; just prior to the 1902 merger it was known as the Indiana, Decatur & Western, and as noted above, afterward it was the western part of the Cincinnati, Indianapolis & Western that in 1902 was leased to the CH&D.

Figure 2.15 The Baltimore & Ohio, a major eastern road, was one of the lesser roads serving Indianapolis. On a sunny day in 1963, B&O E-8A number1435 (in the "sunburst" paint scheme) and mates are pointed west on Union Station's track 5. B&O passenger service ended in 1950, so this would have been a special run, unfortunately not identified by the photographer.

Ron Stuckey photo, John Fuller collection

All B&O passenger service ended in 1950, but Amtrak's *Cardinal* has used this line since 1986 for the Cincinnati–Indianapolis portion of its route. Most of the line west of Indianapolis has been abandoned. Approaching from the southeast, the B&O came into Indianapolis along the north side of U.S. Route 52 and south of the PRR line to Union Station. To the west, the line diverged from Union Station and Big Four trackage and ran northwest a little south of the Indianapolis Motor Speedway.

Nickel Plate Road (New York, Chicago & St. Louis Railway)

The Nickel Plate (NKP) was a major player in Indiana, its 773 route miles constituting around 10 percent of the state's total in the early twentieth century. In Indianapolis its presence was modest, although its predecessor line was among the city's earliest rail routes. The Peru & Indianapolis Railroad was chartered in 1846 and extended from Indianapolis to Peru by 1854. Briefly operated by the PRR predecessor Madison & Indianapolis Railroad, the line was reorganized in 1864 as the Indianapolis, Peru & Chicago Railway (IP&C) and was leased for a time to a predecessor of the Wabash Railroad. The IP&C was sold in 1887 to the Lake Erie &

Western Railway (LE&W), which merged with the NKP in 1923. The Norfolk & Western Railway acquired the NKP in 1964 and is now an operating unit of Norfolk Southern Corporation. East of Union Station, the LE&W/NKP turned sharply north and ran on a direct route to Tipton, Kokomo, and Michigan City. It ran parallel to and on the east side of the Monon until the two lines diverged around 33rd Street, just south of the NKP's North Yard.

Monon Railroad (Chicago, Indianapolis & Louisville Railway)

The Monon was better known by its nickname than by its corporate one, and in 1956 the nickname became the corporate name. Also called "the Monon Route" and "the Hoosier Line," this was Indiana's own railroad. If states had adopted railroads as mascots, the Monon would have been Indiana's. Fifth largest in the state, the Monon had an early start but was late arriving in Indianapolis. Chartered as the New Albany & Salem Railroad (NA&S) in 1847, it succeeded an unbuilt line proposed in the Mammoth Internal Improvement Act. From New Albany on the Ohio River, the line reached Salem by 1851 and Crawfordsville by 1854. It then ran to Lafayette on an existing line. Another railroad starting from Michigan City had reached Lafayette in 1853, so by 1854 the NA&S connected the Ohio River with Lake Michigan.

Renaming the line the Louisville, New Albany & Chicago Railroad (LNA&C) in 1859 showed its intent to reach the Windy City. As a result, the little White County town of Bradford, later renamed Monon (derived from a Potawatomi word), became the railroad's focal point. In 1878 the narrow-gauge Indianapolis, Delphi & Chicago Railroad connected Monon and Rensselaer; it was converted to standard gauge in 1881, whereupon the LNA&C acquired it and built onward toward Chicago; it never actually reached the center of that city but instead relied on trackage rights. The company also built southeast to Indianapolis in 1883. The LNA&C entered receivership and reorganized in 1897 as the Chicago, Indianapolis & Louisville Railway; it emerged from another nearly thirteen-year receivership in 1946, and in 1956 the corporate name became Monon Railroad. Sold in 1971 to the Louisville & Nashville Railroad, the Monon ended up in the CSX Transportation fold.

In Indianapolis the Monon line ran east from Union Station and turned north to parallel the NKP on the west. It then ran into Hamilton County and turned northwest toward Frankfort and Monon. Much of it has been abandoned, although Amtrak uses part of the northern portion for trains between Chicago and Indianapolis. In Indianapolis, part of the former Monon roadbed makes up the 18.5-mile Monon Trail, along which the railroad's heritage is celebrated in various ways.

Illinois Central Railroad

Among the last built of the capital city's railroad lines is the former Illinois Central (IC). It had 175 route miles in Indiana, all of them branches from the main line between Chicago and New Orleans. The branch from Effingham, Illinois, to Indianapolis began service in 1880 as a narrow-gauge line between Effingham and Switz City, Indiana. It suffered financial reverses, was converted to standard gauge in 1887, and purchased by the IC in 1900. With the financial support of the IC, the Indianapolis Southern Railway was extended to Indianapolis in 1906 and was absorbed into the IC in 1909. The line is famous for the Richland Creek Viaduct, better known as Tulip Trestle, nearly 2,300 feet long and, at 157 feet, the highest railroad bridge in Indiana, carrying the daily traffic of the Indiana Rail Road (INRD). This company was formed in 1986 when the IC had plans to abandon its Indianapolis

Figure 2.17 For its freight traffic the Monon had a modest engine terminal at its 27th Street yard north of downtown Indianapolis. In the summer of 1968, living on borrowed time, several of the road's venerable cab units doze in the sun while awaiting the call to duty.

Jay Williams/Big Four Graphics collection

line. Now a prosperous regional railroad owning or operating over more than 500 route miles, the INRD, headquartered in Indianapolis, is a major player in Indiana freight hauling. The company provides service over its own lines and, by means of trackage and haulage rights, to and from Chicago and Louisville. The line has been majority-owned by CSX since 1995 but is maintained as a separate operation.

The IC line approached Indianapolis from the south, skirting the east bank of the White River south of Raymond Street before entering a small yard today known as the Senate Avenue Yard. The line continued north just west of Senate Avenue and turned east to join the Union Station trackage west of the train shed. That portion north of the Senate Avenue Yard was abandoned some time ago.

Growing Pains

Filling in the Indianapolis railroad map was a long process, spanning the years from 1847 to 1918. But even by the early 1880s the railroads were feeling growing pains: too many tracks, too many trains, too many freight cars to handle, too many passengers to move around and keep happy. These were good growing pains, symptoms of a wildly successful railroad network that made a huge contribution to the growth, wealth, and ongoing development of Indianapolis. At the same time, the railroads and the city were tripping over each other: the railroads had trouble dealing with their ever-increasing freight and passenger traffic, and so did the city; too many trains in the downtown area significantly impeded pedestrian and vehicular traffic. The solution would require creative thinking and a large investment in two groundbreaking and innovative undertakings.

Notes

1. *Ohio State Journal*, February 25, 1850. Emphasis in original. No page indicated, no volume or number. Photocopy of newspaper page.

2. W. R. Holloway, *Indianapolis*, 324.

3. Paxson, "The Railroads of the 'Old Northwest' before the Civil War," n.p.

4. *American Railway Guide* (New York: Curran Dinsmore & Co., 1852), 2.

5. "The Value and Importance of Railroads," in William Prescott Smith, ed., *The Book of the Great Railway Celebrations of 1857* (New York: D. Appleton & Co., 1858), 176–7.

6. *A Chronology of American Railroads* (Washington, DC: Association of American Railroads, 1962), 7.

7. See the Conexus Indiana website: http://www.conexusindiana.com/overview.

8. Victor M. Bogle, "Railroad Building in Indiana, 1850–1855," *Indiana Magazine of History* 58, no. 3 (September 1962): 221.

9. *Chronology of American Railroads*, 7.

10. Barrows and Darbee, "Urban Frontier," 263.

11. Most pioneer American railroads, through various reorganizations, leases, sales, and other transactions, ended up as components of larger railroad systems, usually before the end of the nineteenth century. The corporate evolution of each of the lines serving Indianapolis is an intriguing story in itself but will not be covered in detail here because it has been so well documented in Richard Simons and Francis Parker's *Railroads of Indiana*, published by Indiana University Press in 1997. Well-organized, authoritative, and readable, this book traces every important segment of every Indiana railroad from inception to ultimate disposition. It provided the basic facts for the descriptions of Indianapolis railroads in this chapter.

3

THE UNION

ON ANY GIVEN DAY, Indianapolis International Airport is a bustling scene of cars, buses, vans, taxis, arriving and departing flights, and crowds of people. Inside the terminal, ticket agents serve lines of passengers, baggage is tagged and sent on its way, and waiting areas are full of travelers. Now imagine that same activity transported to Indianapolis Union Station in the heart of downtown Indianapolis and backdated some eight or nine decades. It might be difficult to visit that silent landmark now and realize what a nexus of trade, commerce, and social interaction it was at one time. Union Station in its prime, though, was just as important to the city as the airport is today, except that Union Station's vitality, its hum of commerce, its buzzing activity, and its excitement diffused outward into the surrounding cityscape, enlarging and enhancing the social and commercial life of Indianapolis in a way the airport cannot.

MAKING TRACKS

As early railroads targeted Indianapolis, the city's movers and shakers made a far-sighted decision that had a significant impact on the visual character and physical form of the community.

Most of the early railroads of Indiana were small regional undertakings, but their tracks typically ended in "destination" or terminal cities such as Indianapolis with the expectation that they would connect with other lines to other places. Over time, the majority of Indianapolis railroads would approach from the east and west, with a smaller number coming in from north and south. In the Midwest, the earliest lines sought to connect established Great Lakes and Ohio and Mississippi river routes to the interior. Soon, though, new rail routes ran east–west to permit connections with growing eastern trunk lines. This happened early on in Indianapolis, in the era immediately preceding the Civil War, when railroad builders sought connections to New York City, Philadelphia, and Baltimore to the east and Chicago and St. Louis to the west, placing Indianapolis along many of the most direct routes.

Enthusiasm for the new travel mode often triggered anticipatory commercial development. Holloway's 1870 Indianapolis history, for example, captured the era in an account that sounded like a report from an excited eyewitness rather than a historian writing more than twenty years later:

The Madison Railroad was now coming so close to the town, that its impulse was felt in business; and the first throbbings of the energy which was to develop such great results, began to stir the little county town with the hopes of greatness and prosperity which the visit of the "Robert Hanna" created and disappointed. The Company had selected its depot-ground on South street, east of Pennsylvania, then clear out of town. But the ground was high, and cheap, and convenient; and the first angry complaints of the citizens at this mislocation, soon died out in the bustle and excitement of the actual arrival of the road in 1847. The depot would not come to the town, so the town went to the depot,—planted heavy business houses all around it, and created, for a time, a sort of commercial center there. The creek was straightened from Virginia Avenue to Meridian street, by the property holders, and the streets graded and filled across the low muddy space of the creek "bottom."[1]

Cross-currents were at work here: the first railroad neared the city; the business community and the citizenry were wildly excited; the railroad company selected a convenient and inexpensive depot site outside the developed part of town; the town was annoyed at first but all was forgiven; and the community responded to the economic stimulus of the railroad by creating a new commercial district focused on the depot, shifting the city's commercial core southward. As Holloway noted, this shift endured only "for a time"; as other railroads passed north of the M&I's terminus, development moved northward again. However, as late as the mid-1870s, city maps showed a concentration of commercial buildings in the blocks near the M&I's original depot. Though the density and intensity of development did move back north, the southern part of downtown Indianapolis, southward from South Street, had already been marked as the locus of mainly commercial and industrial rather than residential development, and it would stay that way.

THE UNION STATION IDEA

As the nation's railroad network grew in the nineteenth century, in large towns and small, competing railroads often built separate passenger depots. At the time, this made sense: why share a depot with another railroad and make it easier for your competitor to siphon off your passenger, mail, telegraph, and express traffic? In smaller towns, this was not much of an inconvenience for passengers needing to change railroads. In the larger cities, it was a much more significant issue.

Two examples: In Cincinnati and Chicago the various railroads built individual passenger depots, often many blocks apart. In both the Queen City and the windy one, many passengers were forced to transfer between the separate depots. Indeed, Chicago was the poster child for this problem. Until 1969, all six of its major passenger depots were in operation.[2] There were various plans over the years to build a single large depot, but costs and logistical issues stymied them all. The problem would not be solved until Amtrak in the 1970s gathered all its intercity routes at Union Station. Regional commuters, however, must still use several different depots. Cincinnati's solution was the architecturally brilliant Cincinnati Union Terminal, a state-of-the-art facility when it opened in 1933, but even it had the flaw of being located well outside the city core, where it was inaccessible on foot and the intended streetcar service to it was never completed.

So would Indianapolis travelers be similarly inconvenienced? Yes and no. Even when only the Madison & Indianapolis served the city, it was widely recognized that numerous other lines were abuilding, each desiring its own facility. Two of these railroads even proposed laying tracks in city streets to reach the central area of town. The Peru & Indianapolis and the Indianapolis & Bellefontaine roads pushed this idea, but due to considerable opposition decided instead to skirt the undeveloped eastern side of the Mile Square and then turn southwest along Pogue's Run to a connection with the tracks of the Madison & Indianapolis.[3]

Witold Rybczynski's book about Frederick Law Olmsted, quoted in chapter 1, discusses the relationship between railroads and the cities they served, noting that street patterns and building lot plats seldom allowed for the introduction of railroads. No space was set aside for tracks, depots, shops, or the myriad other physical facilities needed by railroads. Not surprisingly, and as was the case in Indianapolis, this was because many communities were laid out well before the concept of the railroad had been developed well enough for town planners to foresee its impact. As Rybczynski notes, "Planning rail lines and streets simultaneously was unusual in the nineteenth century; tracks were typically laid long after the streets were built, requiring expensive expropriation and causing disruption of the city fabric and traffic."[4] The result was that tracks and facilities often had to be shoehorned into the existing setting, making life difficult for both the railroad and the city it served.

In the early railroad years of Indianapolis, this was not a significant problem. Residential and commercial development in the city was first concentrated on an east–west axis a block south of Monument Circle. By 1835 the developed area had increased at least fourfold, but it extended only a block and a half to the south. Most development had occurred in an area between three and four blocks to the north and east of the Circle. Almost tripling in size by 1850, the developed area by then extended up to six blocks or more to the west, north, and east (remember the tendency for development to occur toward the *upstream* end of local waterways), but only about four blocks to the south. However, one lobe of development at this time had pushed another three blocks southward and was centered around the Madison & Indianapolis tracks and terminal, as recounted in Holloway's history, suggesting that the anticipated economic benefits of the railroad outweighed any negative influences from whatever might be floating in Pogue's Run.[5]

The result was that the seven rail lines completed in Indianapolis in the pre–Civil War period found it easy to avoid settled areas of expensive land. They could locate close to those areas without undue disruption of the urban fabric, with the southern portion of the Mile Square the most logical place to enter the city. Soon, though, continued growth and increases in street and rail traffic would make the location of the railroads an issue to be reckoned with.

The Indianapolis Union Railway Company

It quickly became apparent to the city fathers and the business community that additional railroads would likely want their own separate depots and might also want to occupy city streets. In addition to blocking traffic in these streets, the sheer quantity of trackage, the density of traffic, and the multiplicity of routes for inbound, outbound, and through passengers posed a serious potential problem. The railroads did in fact build separate depots;

as early as 1852 there were seven in operation or proposed. As shown on a railroad map of the city published that year,[6] these depots formed a crescent around the city. At the northeast, the Indianapolis & Bellefontaine had a depot along Massachusetts Avenue, northeast of the Mile Square; the Peru & Indianapolis (P&I) had one on East Street a block south of Washington; that of the "Lawrenceburg" (the Indianapolis & Cincinnati) was at East Street, a block south of Washington; and that of the "Madison" (the Madison & Indianapolis) at South and Pennsylvania. The "General Passenger Depot" was shown along the south edge of Louisiana Street between Meridian and Illinois, while the "Terre Haute" depot (the Terre Haute & Richmond) was two blocks to the west. Finally, on the northwest side of town, just outside the Mile Square and just west of Mississippi Street (later Senate Avenue) was the depot of the Lafayette & Indianapolis. Left unaddressed, this trend toward widely separated depots would have created a real inconvenience comparable to that in Chicago—but that "General Passenger Depot" shown on the 1852 map would change everything.

Indianapolis is rightly credited with being the first to conceive the idea of a common depot unifying all its railroads' passenger services—a "union" depot—so patrons would not have to slog through rain, snow, and mud, or have to hunt down hansom cabs or buggies to make baggage-laden transfers between depots. (For a discussion of what city had the first union station building, see the sidebar "Union Station: Who Was First?") Though shown on the 1852 map, the unifying depot would not be completed until late in 1853. Once it was, the logic of accommodating all the city's passenger trains there was so compelling that the

Union Station: Who Was First?

The citizens of Indianapolis are justifiably proud of their handsome and historic Union Station, and also of the claim that when its predecessor opened for service in 1853 it was the nation's first union station. It should be noted, though, that some citizens of the next state capital to the east would like to tell Indianapolis "Not so fast." They would point out that there is good reason to believe that the first union station of Columbus, Ohio predated that of Indianapolis. The capital of the Buckeye State is a fine place, but it suffers occasional bouts of self-doubt, so matters such as this can be of some import.

Assuming for argument's sake that Indianapolis has a sound claim to its position, but that Columbus's claim is also legitimate, what should we conclude? A review of the historical record leads to an answer frequently employed by historians of many stripes: It depends.

The facts are pretty straightforward and well documented. The railroads of Indianapolis, both those already operating and those under construction, cooperated in 1849 to create both a union railway company and a union depot company, thus establishing when the already-conceived idea of a "union" passenger facility was actually formalized. Construction then took another four years or so, with the new Union Depot opening in 1853.

Over in Columbus the city's first rail route was the Columbus & Xenia (C&X), which connected with the Little Miami Railroad at Xenia to provide through service between Cincinnati and the capital city. In early 1850 the C&X entered Columbus from the southwest and terminated temporarily at a depot on the west side of the Scioto River, across from the downtown area. Late in that same year, with a river bridge completed, the C&X was extended eastward another half mile or so to terminate in a barn-like wood depot just east of North High Street at the northern edge of the city's downtown area. As in Indianapolis, this depot, owned by the C&X, was a "through" rather than a "stub" depot, with three tracks that ran through the building from southwest to northeast. It was designed that way because the railroad from Cleveland, the Cleveland, Columbus & Cincinnati (CC&C), was nearing completion and intended to connect with the C&X and become a tenant of the C&X depot. Indeed the CC&C, which was an entirely separate corporate entity from the C&X, entered the city in 1851, connected with the C&X, used the depot, and was part of the three-railroad line that provided through-car service between Cleveland, Columbus, and Cincinnati. So by 1851 Columbus had a railroad depot that was a de facto "union" depot that served two different railroad companies. By this measure, Columbus had a union depot a good two years before Indianapolis.

Which city can rightly claim the earlier union depot depends on how the argument is framed. Columbus had a functioning union depot two years before Indianapolis, but that depot was owned by a single railroad and used by another as a tenant. The union depot in Indianapolis was built later than the one in Columbus, but the concept of a union depot, which was the product of cooperation among several railroads that all had an ownership stake in both the depot and the tracks serving it, dated from 1848 (when the city ordinance was passed authorizing such a depot) or 1849 (when the railroads agreed to proceed) or 1850 (when the Union Track Railway Company was formed with the charge of building a union depot). The "union" concept went beyond one railroad owning a depot and letting another use it, and the idea was well established in Indianapolis by the time the first railroad entered Columbus.

Regardless of how one interprets the historical record, or on which side of the record one comes down, one thing is not open to dispute: Indianapolis has been wise enough, through thick and thin, to hang on to Union Station rather than giving up and knocking it down. In contrast, Columbus demolished its Union Station in 1977 to make way for a convention center of a widely unloved architectural design. Only a single arch from its ornate entrance arcade has been preserved in a nearby park.

Advantage, Indianapolis.

individual depots were quickly abandoned by their respective companies.

Who was first to propose this idea may be lost to history (Sulgrove's 1884 history of Indianapolis credits General Thomas Armstrong with the concept), but the city took to the idea. Just before Christmas of 1848, the Common Council of Indianapolis passed an ordinance allowing creation of a union railway company to build and operate trackage, and a union depot company to build and operate a depot. Thus was born an idea that would shape future rail travel in Indianapolis and across the nation.[7]

After another year passed (the capital-intensive railroads tended to be deliberate decision makers when it came to new investment), several railroads were ready to act. On December 19, 1849, representatives of four railroad companies adopted the following resolution: "Resolved, that it is expedient to locate and establish at Indianapolis a joint railroad track, connecting the Madison and Indianapolis, the Terre Haute and Richmond, the Peru and Indianapolis, and the Indianapolis and Bellefontaine railroads. And to locate and establish on said joint track a joint passenger depot for said joint companies."[8]

On April 1, 1850, the Common Council passed an ordinance authorizing track construction rather than just the formation of an entity that would be able to do so. The P&I having partially withdrawn in the meantime, on May 31, 1850, the three remaining railroads formed the Union Track Railway Company ("union" apparently sounded better than "joint") to operate tracks connecting the participating roads. This was an unincorporated entity to which the participants donated tracks they built at their own expense. The tracks were quickly completed, by June 19,

1850, and included a segment originally built as part of its line by the P&I. The company chose, however, not to help build the first Union Depot because it disagreed with the depot's proposed location.[9]

A summary of this earliest of the entities that led to construction of the city's two union stations includes the following:

ORGANIZATION: Organized at a meeting of the Presidents of Madison and Indianapolis Railroad Company, The Terre Haute and Richmond Railroad Company, and Indianapolis and Bellefontaine Railroad Company held May 31, 1850, at which Chauncey Rose was chosen President and Colonel T.A. Morris, Constructing Engineer and Treasurer. The President of the Peru & Indianapolis Railroad Company was subsequently admitted to the Board of Directors but, being dissatisfied with the location of the station, that Company decided not to bear its share of the cost of the station grounds and construction and did not use the property until January, 1854. On November 25, 1852, the Directors adopted a resolution prescribing the terms under which other railroad companies might be admitted to the union arrangement by paying their equal proportion of the cost of the station grounds, buildings, tracks and right-of-way. Lawrenceburg and Upper Mississippi Railroad Company was admitted to membership November 25, 1852,[10] and the Indiana Central Railway Company and Lafayette and Indianapolis Railroad Company were admitted to membership in 1854.

CHANGE OF NAME: The name of the Company was changed to The Indianapolis Union Railway Company by resolution of the Board of Directors adopted August 12, 1853.

UNION DEPOT, INDIANAPOLIS.

Figure 3.1 This west end view of the first Union Depot, likely made not long after its 1853 completion, has been widely published. Unfortunately, no photos of the building are so far known to exist. The Italianate design—tower, arched openings, eave brackets—is apparent; also note the destination signs over the tracks. Surrounding business buildings have already been constructed; one is marked "Offices, Bellefontaine R.R. Co."

Indiana Historical Society, P0211

TERMINI AND DESCRIPTION (At date of Change of Name): The purpose of the union was to connect the four railways first above mentioned under 'Organization,' then completed, or about to be completed, into Indianapolis, control the operation of the connecting track, and the construction and operation of a union station. The union tracks extended from Tennessee Street [now Capitol Avenue] on the west, to the north line of New York Street on the northeast, 1.38 miles, with a west connection leading to the Madison and Indianapolis Railroad, 0.13 of a mile, and an east connection with that road, 0.09 of a mile, a total of 1.60 miles, all in Indianapolis, Indiana. The Union Station was located between Meridian and Illinois Streets.

In November 1852 the company passed a resolution establishing requirements for other railroads to join the "union arrangement." Each was required to pay its proportional share of the costs of operating and maintaining the Union Railway and the Union Depot.[11] The Indianapolis Union Railway Company eventually was incorporated in November 1872 under state legislation that legalized the existence of union railroad companies.

1853: UNION DEPOT

The Union Tracks were a prelude to construction of the union depot the city had authorized and the railroad companies had committed to build. The Union Railway undertook this effort on its own without establishing the separate union depot company the enabling ordinance had allowed but not required. Not long after the Union Tracks were completed in mid-1850, a "joint committee" representing the participating railroads chose a depot site: the northern half of Square 96 of the 1821 Indianapolis plat. Louisiana Street was the north boundary, and Meridian and Illinois streets were, respectively, the east and west boundaries. The north wall of the depot was to be set fifteen feet south of Louisiana Street; however, despite earlier objections to construction of railroads in city streets, the freight tracks along the depot's north side appear to have taken up a good part of Louisiana from Meridian Street all the way to West Street. Of course there were public objections, not to encroachment upon Louisiana Street but to the depot's location. The citizenry felt it was too far south of Washington Street, which was the alignment of the National Road and was considered the south edge of the community.[12] There can be no doubt, however, that had the depot site been proposed farther north, a howl of public protest would also have arisen because, with all its crowds, noise, and smoke, it would have been too *close* to the center of town.

Some sources say that English architect Joseph Curzon, who was working in Indianapolis, designed the new depot; others suggest that General Armstrong and Colonel Morris, strong promoters of the "union" concept, did the design and construction and that Curzon likely designed only the 1866 south side addition.[13]

So far no photos of the depot seem to have surfaced even though it was a major Indianapolis building of its era. Possibly photos have been lost or are in a collection unknown to researchers. In any case, verbal descriptions and artists' renderings are all we have to understand how Union Depot looked.

Although railroad depots were an entirely new building type, the Indianapolis depot's design was thoroughly consistent with the architectural conventions of the time. Italianate in style, it had the hallmarks (what architectural historians call "character-defining features") of that mid-nineteenth-century design mode: rectangular and arched window and door openings with vertical proportions; bracketed roof eaves and eave returns; and a feeling of verticality achieved through a steeply pitched gable roof with even steeper cross gables, a monitor at the peak of the main roof, and a tall central tower. Construction of Union Depot began in 1852, and it opened for service on September 20, 1853. It rested on a stone foundation and was of brick bearing wall construction. Although no confirmation has been found, we can assume that the interior structure was of wood in this pre-iron-and-steel period. Large trusses would have supported the roof, a technology well known at the time due to decades of American experience in wood bridge-building. The roof's height and pitch suggest that the trusses spanned the width of the building, leaving the track and platform area clear of columns.

The depot was built at ground level, a logical decision at the time but one that would require massive corrective work. Tracks extending west of the depot curved north to join the freight bypass tracks and then diverged into the routes of the participating railroads, all of which crossed the White River on their own

Figure 3.2 An eastward view from somewhat later, perhaps around 1870, shows how the presence of the railroad and the depot stimulated commercial development along the north side of Louisiana Street.

Indiana Historical Society, P0211

Main Passenger Railroad Station, Union Depot, Indianapolis.

bridges. Tracks east of the depot had to deal with Pogue's Run; both the main tracks and the wye to the Madison & Indianapolis were on low trestles. Although various segments of the run were covered up over time, it would not be fully enclosed until the World War I era, at the beginning of the track elevation project that would finally raise the tracks above street level.

The result of the efforts of the "Union" railroads was, for its time, a stylish and serviceable depot. It measured around 50,000 square feet, placing close to an acre and a quarter under roof. Trains passed through five arched openings in the east and west ends of the building. Descriptions of its dimensions vary, but they average around 125 by 400 feet, so that it could accommodate six to eight of the era's passenger cars on each track. Above the entry arches, the end walls had five large circular openings, presumably unglazed so locomotive smoke could be blown away by passing breezes. The rooftop monitor provided some natural light for

Figure 3.3 At the east end of Union Depot, low trestles carried tracks over the swampy land along Pogue's Run. In a view looking west, an artist's rendering shows some industrial development south of the tracks, with commercial development on the north, a pattern that would persist well into the twentieth century.

Indiana Historical Society, Bass Photo Co. Collection

what must have been a somewhat gloomy train shed, and it also probably helped clear out accumulated smoke.

Lettering on the entry arches spelled out what some historians have described as the names of the railroads that used the depot. However, judging from various artists' views, the lettering actually indicated the principal destinations of the trains on each track. The central arch, for example, was lettered "Dayton," which was neither the corporate nor the informal name of any of the city's railroads at the time, nor was the "Cleveland & Pittsburgh" on an adjacent arch. Indeed, in an era when the name of a railroad could be expected to change every other Wednesday, to direct patrons to the right track it made better sense to indicate destinations rather than railroad names.

Contemporary images of Union Depot also suggested its salutary effects on the city. Crowds of people were shown wandering about the grounds and standing on the tracks as trains approached. Presumably they moved out of the way in time, but their presence was evidence that the depot drew people to it, and the crowds were a stimulus to economic development. Even though Union Depot was not in the city's heart, in these views three- and four-story buildings can be seen around the open ground north of the depot, along the west side of Illinois Street, and along the east side of Meridian. These were business buildings, occupied by enterprises that wanted to be close to the new transportation mode; in time, the area became known as—and still is—the Wholesale District of Indianapolis. So Union Depot was a real plus from both an economic development and an urban planning point of view. It concentrated and organized the city's rail passenger service; it facilitated commerce and trade through its ability to move people, goods, mail, express shipments, money, and important documents quickly and safely; and it stimulated investment in the physical fabric of Indianapolis. More intangibly but no less importantly, it heightened the city's sense of importance, as a locus of modernity and vision that could claim its place among the growing population centers of the Midwest.

Historian John H. White argued that the new depot represented a turning point: "Union Depot appears to have been the first to collect all the major rail lines entering a city and put them in one building. The building was hardly a marble palace, nor did it likely spend much in the way of gilt ornamentation. It was just a great barn . . . a cheap commercial structure built for a purpose rather than a look. Here, passengers could change trains for destinations throughout the area just by walking between platforms."[14] A little harsh, perhaps, since the depot represented an effort to work within the design conventions of the time and create a building with some architectural character. But White had a point: here was something completely new that would have a lasting and beneficial effect on the city.

The depot garnered positive reviews. Images of the interior seem to be non-existent, but the *Railroad Record* of October 27, 1853, painted a word picture: "The Union Passenger Depot Indianapolis, is now occupied by the different companies that built it. There are five tracks in it, the Terre Haute, the Bellefontaine, the Central, the Madison, and the Lawrenceburg, with a convenient platform between each. The rooms for the ladies are splendidly furnished, with every convenience, and the gentlemen have large and comfortable rooms. This is an excellent arrangement, and would be all the better if it were extended to accommodate all the

Union Depot & American Hotel.

Figure 3.4 A southwest view along the north side of Union Depot notes that an early hotel was built nearby (almost out of view to the right). Hotels were naturally attracted to rail depots: by the early twentieth century Indianapolis could boast the Washington, the Severin, and the Barnes, to name just a few that were close to the Union Tracks.

Indiana Historical Society, Bass Photo Co. Collection

roads running into the city."[15] There apparently was no dining room, but an "eating house" was added in 1866.[16] Note, however, that within a few weeks of the depot's opening this observer was already suggesting that the depot should be enlarged. It is also worth noting that the term "Union Depot" more commonly referred to the first depot of 1853; "Union Station" was the name for its 1888 replacement. Technically a station is any named point along a railroad line, regardless of whether there is a building at that location; a depot (sometimes called a "terminal") is the building itself.

Union Depot did have some notable limitations. The freight tracks bypassing the building were on its north side, where freight trains would have hampered foot and vehicle traffic between the depot and the heart of the city. Grade-level trackage also interfered with traffic on the cross streets, a situation only slightly relieved by the construction in 1872 of the Illinois Street tunnel under the tracks. The depot tracks were all at grade as well, along with the platforms by which passengers reached them. Passengers often had to walk across tracks to board their trains, and if a track was blocked, they had to climb over the steps and platforms of the cars in their way. Historical images show no evidence of fencing or anything else to control pedestrians idling about on the Union's tracks; over time the increase in train traffic and in the number of people in or near the station became a real safety issue. Finally, the depot's design did not allow for easy expansion of its train shed, the tracks, or the passenger facilities in the building. What became most intolerable about the 1853 depot, though, was that it quickly proved too small to handle the passengers and trains it was hosting. From some 76 trains a day in 1870—that in

itself a large increase from the number served on opening day seventeen years before—traffic had grown by an even hundred, to 176 a day, by the mid-1880s. Something had to be done.

1888: UNION STATION

We have the federal government to thank—and specifically the now-defunct Interstate Commerce Commission (ICC)—for our ability today to find in primary source documents a detailed picture of what the nation's railroads looked like nearly a century ago. The period around World War I was something of a golden age for American railroads, a time when the nation's rail network was at its greatest, the number of passenger trains was at its peak, and there was little or no competition from other travel modes for passenger and freight traffic (even from the electric interurban lines, which were also at their peak). Ironically, this was also a time when nearly 20 percent of rail mileage was owned or operated by railroads in receivership, and when the railroads got a large black eye for failing to move World War I matériel efficiently. Indeed, the federal government had found it necessary to take over the railroads and run them itself for a while in order to get adequate supplies to the Allied armies fighting in Europe.

This was nothing new. At one time or another nearly everyone hated the railroads for some reason, and they were the primary villains of the late-nineteenth-century "robber baron" era. Early in the twentieth century there was a strong belief that the railroads were heavily overcapitalized (and some good evidence that they were). In response, the ICC required the railroads to prepare detailed inventories of their systems to permit valuation

of their physical assets. The result was an astoundingly complete (and complex) body of information documenting the railroads down to their last nut, bolt, and tie. A vast cornucopia of maps, photos, drawings, histories, and inventory sheets came out of this effort, most of which ended up in the National Archives, but some can also be found in various public and private collections.

Many of the valuation materials covering the 1888 Union Station are available, and they are a rich source of information. One document in particular, a typewritten narrative, provides detailed information about both Union Station and the track elevation project of the early twentieth century. This document provided much of the information for the following narrative.[17]

A Fresh Start

Regardless of whether the city fathers, the traveling public, or the railroads of the city could see it coming, the tremendous growth of railroad passenger traffic in Indianapolis from the early 1850s to the early 1880s was a plain fact, as was the inadequacy of the 1853 Union Depot in serving this traffic. Inconvenience affected not only the passengers using the depot but also the railroad companies themselves. Congestion and delays threw schedules out of kilter, increased costs, and reduced revenues, leaving no one satisfied with the situation.

James McCrea, who would serve as president of the mighty Pennsylvania Railroad (PRR) between 1907 and 1912 (and who, during that time, brought the massive Pennsylvania Station project to fruition in New York City), was manager of the PRR's Southwest System in the early 1880s and general manager of Lines West in 1885. He is credited as the prime mover in the development of a new union station for Indianapolis.[18] Hetherington quotes an 1886 *Indianapolis Journal* article praising McCrea's leadership: "The fact is that nothing would have been done for years to come about a new union depot . . . but for Mr. McCrea's persistent urging the matter. . . . The *Journal* has the best of authority for saying that the first time he met the board of directors, he brought the matter up, and there has not been a meeting since which he attended that the subject of a new union depot has not been discussed." Directors of the Indianapolis Union Railway

responded by passing a resolution at the end of 1884 to get moving on the project. McCrea may also have influenced the choice of the new depot's architect, Thomas Rodd of Pittsburgh. Rodd was employed by the Pennsylvania Railroad but also took other commissions.

Since the new depot and associated track and structures would take up much more space than the original, land acquisition, vacating of streets, and legislation and other legal matters had to be dealt with before the dirt could fly. Cooperation by the City of Indianapolis was readily forthcoming, enabling McCrea to report that "the city authorities have acted very honorably with the company, in fact granting them all the favors they expected, and the Union Railway Company now has good titles to every piece of property between Meridian and Illinois Streets, both north and south of the Union Depot, which they need."[19]

The much-needed depot built between 1886 and 1888 was not just a single building; it was a multi-component improvement that would give Indianapolis an up-to-date transportation facility capable of serving the city for the foreseeable future, though it would turn out that the foreseeable future was fairly brief. The constituent parts of Union Station were listed as follows in the ICC document: "Beginning in November, 1886, additional facilities were provided consisting of a rearranged and enlarged track system, renewed and additional retaining walls along Pogue's Run, new bridge over Pogue's Run, head house and office building, trainshed, east and west baggage buildings, and double track streetcar tunnel in Illinois Street, sidewalk and street paving and ornamental plats at north approach to the station." The "tunnel in Illinois Street" was an improvement of the existing 1872 bore;

Figure 3.6 Though heavily retouched, this 1903 photo, which looks southeast, shows the 1888 Union Station largely in its original condition. The urban scene, though, has changed. Electric streetcars now take people throughout the city, and Jackson Place has been landscaped with a driveway and oval-shaped planting beds. Behind Union Station is its original arched train shed, which had a gable-roofed entry bay above the Illinois Street tunnel.

Indiana Historical Society,
Bass Photo Co. Collection

the "ornamental plats" on the north side referred to what became known as Jackson Place, named for William N. Jackson, a long-time employee at both union depots who was remembered for his many services to travelers.[20]

The "head house and office building" was, of course, the building we call Union Station. Note, though, that the "trainshed"

(today more commonly rendered as two words) was an element separate from the depot. This was the result of evolution in the design of railroad passenger facilities. In their earliest days, railroads often used existing buildings—a tavern, say, or a commercial building or even a house—as depots. Tracks adjacent to them typically were out in the open, with no weather protection for passengers. When railroads built their own depots, they sometimes included one or two tracks under their roofs. This building form quickly evolved so that, as early as the late 1830s, the covered track area, the "shed," became the most prominent element of the depot, with waiting rooms, ticket offices, and other facilities walled off from the shed (which was not heated) and located on one or both sides of the tracks, often in quite narrow spaces that could be quickly outgrown. The 1853 Union Depot in Indianapolis was just such a building.

The integrated depot/train shed, then, with depot facilities, tracks, and passenger platforms all under a single roof, had become the standard form of the American railroad passenger depot in the period before the Civil War. By contrast, construction of free-standing arched train sheds structurally separate from the depot building began as early as the 1840s in Europe; England and France in particular today still have working early examples of the soaring iron-and-glass sheds that have become the iconic image of European rail travel. This trend did not occur widely in the United States until after the Civil War, when structural iron and steel became widely available and American railroads began building some spectacular train sheds of their own.[21]

Building the depot and the train shed as separate structures had a compelling logic that perhaps was not entirely apparent even to their builders. The depot, as in the case of Indianapolis Union Station, could have several upper floors for offices, since its height was not limited by the height of the shed's roof. In addition, a separate train shed could be expanded—lengthened or widened—more readily than if it had been integrated into the structure of a single building; this was most easily accomplished

simply by building another shed next to the existing one. Finally, again as happened in Indianapolis, the shed could be removed entirely and replaced with a more modern version, even one that could not have been envisioned when the original shed was built.

Because the free-standing arched form of train shed had some undesirable characteristics—lack of temperature control, draftiness, dirt accumulation from locomotive exhaust, often inadequate lighting, high initial and ongoing maintenance expense—its popularity was brief and ended a little after the turn of the twentieth century. This was due at least in part to the widespread introduction of concrete as a building material, which facilitated construction of the umbrella, butterfly, or Bush types of shed.[22] These were less expensive to build and maintain, and they were better ventilated, not to mention cleaner, because of how they vented locomotive exhaust. They employed individual platform roofs just high enough to clear rolling stock, with an open area over each track to carry away the exhaust, while providing passengers and crews protection from the weather.[23] New depots of the era opted for them while, as in Indianapolis, many older depots were retrofitted with them in place of an original arched shed. Yet another means of moving from depot to platform was construction of a concourse over the platforms, with enclosed stairs and ramps down to track level, a design not feasible in Indianapolis.

In the United States today there are only a few surviving examples of the traditional arched train shed. Nine come immediately to mind: Union Station in St. Louis; the Milwaukee Road depot in Minneapolis; the Chicago & North Western/Milwaukee Road depot in Milwaukee; Main Street Station in

Figure 3.7 An impressive array of late-nineteenth-century motive power sits outside the Union Station train shed. These cap-stacked steamers will remain here until just before departure time, when they will back across Meridian Street to couple onto their trains. Having them wait outside the shed reduced smoke and fumes inside it, but doing so required them to uncouple from their trains and move forward to avoid blocking Meridian Street.

Richmond, Virginia; Union Station in Montgomery, Alabama; Mount Royal Station in Baltimore; Reading Terminal in Philadelphia; the Central of Georgia depot in Savannah, Georgia; and the Harrisburg (Pennsylvania) Transportation Center, formerly the Pennsylvania Railroad station, which includes an enclosed concourse with stairs to track level. Only the Milwaukee (built, surprisingly, in 1965) and Harrisburg sheds serve their original purpose; the others are either unused or have new uses. Their associated depots are all in use for various purposes, as are others that have lost their train sheds (the Nashville and Louisville union stations are examples). One additional train shed that could be counted was at the union station in Portland. Maine. The depot was demolished in 1961 but a portion of the train shed has been re-assembled elsewhere in the city.

The new arched train shed in Indianapolis opened for service in 1888, a few weeks after completion of the depot. The shed occupied the site of the demolished 1853 Union Depot and was a sturdy, if undistinguished, example of this type of structure, spanning ten through and two stub tracks. Open on the sides and ends, it was intended to evacuate locomotive smoke quickly, aided by a monitor along the gabled roof's ridge. The steel trusses supporting the roof had a curved lower chord and were supported by latticed steel columns. The shed tended to be dark, though skylights in the roof helped to dispel some of the gloom. There actually were two separate shed structures; the smaller of the two abutted the south wall of the depot building and covered only a few of the tracks; the east and west baggage rooms were built of brick within this shed and stood at its far east and west ends. The larger main shed was built up against the south side of the smaller one and covered the rest of the depot tracks. Both sheds were the same length, something close to a block and a half long (published reports of their dimensions varied but averaged about 300 by 700 feet overall).[24] The freight bypass tracks were relocated to the south side of the train shed, enabling construction of an open plaza in front of the depot's main north entry.

The heart of the project was, of course, the depot itself—Union Station. In this building Indianapolis gained both a modern, for its time, and properly scaled transportation facility, but also a true landmark: it was both a significant addition to the city's architectural wealth and, as a dictionary might define the term, "a prominent and identifying feature of a landscape." In a city that was still primarily low-rise in character, Union Station and its tall clock tower were visible for quite some distance in every direction.

Figure 3.8 Rail traffic at Union Station was at its peak in the early twentieth century, leading to the problem shown in this northwestward view at the east end of the train shed. No fewer than four locomotives are blocking Meridian Street, tying up the commerce of the city and presenting a major safety hazard.

Indiana Historical Society, Bass Photo Co. Collection

In its design, materials, ornamentation, and layout, the new depot building was very much a product of its time. The late Victorian era of the 1880s and 1890s was one of great richness, variety, and eclecticism in architecture, in many ways a culmination of trends that had begun earlier in the century. Although privately owned, Union Station was in every respect a public building—one of the most public in the city, given its function—and as such represented the image, character, and status of the city of Indianapolis. In the late Victorian era, buildings playing this role were intentionally built to be large, impressive, grand, and heavily detailed and ornamented; by this time a rich architectural vocabulary, more complex and drawn from more sources than ever before, was available to Union Station's designer.

Said to have been inspired in part by Pittsburgh's Allegheny County Courthouse, which was built between 1883 and 1888 in a design by Henry Hobson Richardson and with which architect Rodd undoubtedly would have been familiar, Union Station was built in the style named for that giant of American architecture:

Richardsonian Romanesque. Employed most successfully for large buildings with a public function, this mode could be found not only in railroad depots but also in churches, city halls, courthouses, museums, office buildings, and even some large private homes. For railroad companies, this was an era of great effort to build impressive and memorable depots that were advertisements both for the wealth and solidity of the railroads themselves and for the communities they served; as gateways to these cities, the depots played an important civic function that made arrival in and departure from the city a matter of some ceremony. The intent behind showing travelers this level of consideration and respect was to leave them with a favorable impression of both the city and the railroad. This was especially true in larger cities such as Indianapolis. Union Station's clock tower, its massive brick walls, its steep and complicated roofline, its asymmetrical form, and its blend of rectangular and arched window and door openings—all hallmarks of Richardsonian Romanesque—gave it a powerful presence both in the city at large and to those traveling through it.

If Union Station's exterior design imparted a sense of solidity, safety, and permanence, its interior design was intended to impress upon viewers that they were in a place of sophistication, quality, good taste, and excellence. In a word, the interior was a spectacle in the best sense of that word. As the first thing visitors saw upon arrival and the last thing upon departure, it was meant to remain in their minds as the image of Indianapolis. The forms, conventions, and details of the classical architecture of ancient Rome were the inspiration for the interior design. These elements had long been used in architecture, literally for centuries, but

their heyday was the late nineteenth and early twentieth century. Most prominent in Union Station's design was its principal organizing feature, the high barrel-vaulted central space, three stories high and lit by skylights. Huge circular colored-glass windows, evoking the character of a cathedral, dominated the north and south end walls. Arched arcading to either side, located below the balconies that gave access to mezzanine office spaces, opened into the public spaces of the first floor.

The ICC inventory listed the various spaces in the building. The basement had power, heating, and ventilating equipment, a cellar for the restaurant kitchen, and locker rooms for the staff. The first floor had all the public spaces expected of a depot of the era: ticket office, general waiting room (that is, open to everyone), a smoking room and barber shop for men, a separate waiting room for women, and both a lunch room and a more formal dining room. On a mezzanine between the first and second floors were some company offices and, curiously enough, kitchen and pantry spaces. The second and third floors were all devoted to office space, each floor consisting of four large rooms subdivided into smaller spaces by paneling. The attic was unfinished.

Upon the opening of the new Union Station late in 1888, the Indianapolis newspapers were replete with praise for the new temple of transportation. Ranging from simply descriptive to positively rapturous, articles in the city's three papers covered all aspects of the depot and its operations. There were breathless descriptions of the exterior design and of the interior spaces and appointments, of the total expenditures by the Indianapolis Union Railway (IU) to bring the project to fruition, of the scramble to move offices and operations into their new spaces, and of

Figure 3.9 Street traffic crossing the Union Tracks was always a problem, but by 1916 it had become intolerable. What better evidence could there be than this westward view of the Union Station train shed's east end? Every vehicle known to man seems to be trundling up and down Meridian Street while locomotives stand threateningly in the background. It appears that large openings have been cut into the shed's roof to help dissipate the smoke.

*Indiana Historical Society, Bass
Photo Co. Collection*

the effort to accommodate the rush of passengers headed to the State Fair. The ticketing, waiting, lounging, and dining facilities received high praise. Proprietors of nearby businesses joined in the chorus of happy voices. Only a few complaints were aired: failure to build a Meridian Street viaduct, for example, and the absence of offices for the express companies that were forced to use those across the street from the depot. Hetherington's book about Union Station reprints many of these articles and in general paints a thorough picture of the city's response to the facility's completion.

But despite the singing of all these (mostly) praises, the new Indianapolis Union Station inexplicably left unremedied two of the most serious shortcomings of the old Union Depot: the new depot was large, stylish, functional, and well appointed, and its train shed was commodious. But its tracks and platforms were still at grade, still at the level of the surrounding streets, still with no way for passengers to pass over or under the various tracks to get to their trains. This was somewhat mitigated by the railroads' uncoupling their trains to clear the central walkway that crossed the tracks, but this added delays and expense to train operation.

Figure 3.10 A northbound streetcar emerges from the gloom of the Illinois Street tunnel around 1909. The tunnel helped alleviate conflict between Union Station trains and street traffic, but it was far from enough. The Spencer House hotel was one of several that clustered around the station.

Indiana Historical Society, Bass Photo Co. Collection

Then, too, with all the depot tracks still at grade, interference with traffic on city streets continued unabated and promised only to get worse as Indianapolis grew. It was as though the Indianapolis Union Railway had built a larger, more impressive depot that functionally was identical to the badly outdated one from 1853.

Union Station Improvements

Despite all these issues, Union Station did function as intended, even if imperfectly. Trains arrived and departed; passengers arrived and departed; baggage, express shipments, and mail were received and delivered; and rail traffic grew apace as Indianapolis and the nation grew in both size and economic power. Through it all, for over a quarter of a century Union Station remained much as it was originally planned and built.

It was not too long, though, before more complaints arose. Some cited lack of capacity for ever-increasing passenger traffic, since the new facility had only a few more tracks than the one opened in 1853. Some noted vehicle and pedestrian circulation problems around the station area, at the grade crossings in particular. Some claimed that the original interior spaces of the depot no longer worked efficiently. And some no doubt were inspired by the typical American desire for something new once something old has become familiar and a little tiresome.

Perhaps inevitably, only a little more than a decade after the new depot opened there was the beginning of a movement to get the Union Railway to elevate its tracks above street level. At a characteristically deliberate pace, the IU's owners eventually took the first steps in this direction early in the twentieth century. During this same period, probably driven more by practical necessity than by the desire to respond to critics, the IU made various incremental improvements to Union Station, most of them having to do with heating, plumbing, electrical wiring, and toilet facilities; it was not until 1913 that major changes were made to the building.

By that time, pressure from the city's Chamber of Commerce had resulted in establishment of a Track Elevation Commission, which focused its efforts on the elevation project but also promoted improvements to Union Station. Among the ideas put forth was that of building an entirely new depot building. As early as 1910 there was considerable agitation among the business community, the public, and the local press for such an undertaking. Quoting Frank D. Stalnaker, president of the merchants' association, the *Indianapolis Sun* editorialized that "everyone wants a new and larger union station. . . . Citizens of Indianapolis, who have in mind the glory and glorification of Indianapolis; the advertising that a fine union railway station gives, and the fine asset that is found in the first impression a modern union station gives the visitor, are emphatically back of the movement looking to the rebuilding of the old union station on largely expanded lines. . . . Indianapolis ought to put her best foot foremost at her gateway and impress chance comers with her stability, modernity, progressiveness and enterprise."[25]

A lot to expect of a single building, perhaps, but it was clear that the community understood how important a railroad station could be in establishing a city's character, quality, and desirability as a place to live, work, and run a business. Not surprisingly, though, the IU Railway was unmoved by the locals' desire to see it and its member railroads spend money on an entirely new

Figure 3.11 A few blocks north of Union Station, at Illinois and Washington streets, a visitor in 1910 would have found this busy scene. The nation's railroads brought and sustained this level of prosperity.

Indiana Historical Society, Bass Photo Co. Collection

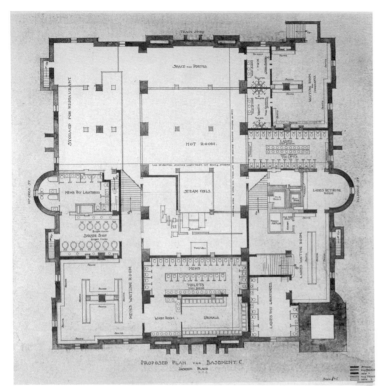

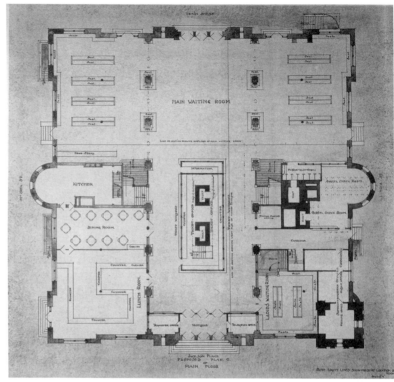

Figures 3.12 and 3.12A In 1913 the Indianapolis Union Railway Company completed interior alterations at Union Station in response to ongoing complaints about its condition. "Plan C" was the design selected for the work, though it appears not to have been implemented entirely as drawn on the basement and first floor plans. The biggest change from the original configuration was placement of the ticket office in the middle of the barrel-vaulted central hall, a move that blocked the expansive view of this space from the north side main entry doors. These drawings are oriented with Jackson Place at the bottom and the south doors into the train shed at the top.

Brian Banta collection

depot. The debate continued for some time but appears to have been put to rest when, on June 3, 1913, Joseph Wood, IU Railway president, wrote to the assistant general secretary of the Chamber of Commerce: "The Directors of the Indianapolis Union Railway Company have given a great deal of thought and study to this question, and believe that, with the improvements consequent on the elevation of the tracks, and the interior remodeling now in progress, the present building will not only be more convenient, but adequate for years to come. . . . It would, in my opinion, be unwise to consider such further large expenditures as would be necessitated by the removal of the present station building and the construction of another."[26]

So the IU would not build anew, but it did agree to make interior improvements, which was done between April 1913 and August 1914 at a cost of $400,000. No doubt the large anticipated costs of the elevation project, planning for which was progressing and for which the initial work would begin in 1915, had much to do with the railroad's position. The city would have to make do with an improved version of the old depot.

The 1913–1914 improvements to Union Station included major changes in the basement, where the floor was lowered more than a foot and, in the west half, an immigrants' room was built (remember this was a period of high immigration from Europe and Eastern Europe to American industrial cities) and women's retiring, waiting, and toilet rooms were fitted out. In the eastern half were a barbershop and men's toilet room, two bathing rooms with tubs, and a smoking room. Separate stairs from the first floor provided access to these new spaces, and the immigrants' room had an exterior stair at the building's southwest corner (note that immigrants did not have interior access to the public spaces on the first floor).

On the first floor, the original women's waiting room and the lunchroom were converted into general waiting room space; this work also removed the Western Union office, the stationmaster's office, and a stair to the balcony. The central doorway out to the train shed was flanked by two new doorways. A newsstand replaced a cigar counter, and the dining room was converted into a smaller dining room, lunchroom, and pantry. The barbershop and men's toilet were turned into additional ticket office space, with a ladies' restroom and toilet adjacent. Increased public telephone and telegraph spaces replaced the smoking room and a custodian's office, and a vault extending to the second floor was built in the tower on the building's northwest corner.

Both railroad traffic trends and social attitudes can be read in this summary of the changes at Union Station: more ticket-selling space, increased phone and telegraph services, and waiting room space for larger crowds of travelers, including foreign immigrants arriving in far larger numbers than in the past who must, it was felt at the time, be separated from "regular" customers; less space for amenities such as dining spaces, presumably because fewer hurrying patrons took the time to stop and eat; and more functional office and operational space for IU staff to keep the whole place working.

Following these major changes, according to the ICC report, numerous other improvements to Union Station were made over the following seven years, including a marquee over the main north side entrance; lavatory, plumbing, heating, and elevator work; and fire escapes and office partitioning. To the IU Railway

Company it must have seemed at times that the needs of the old place would never be met and the work never done. In fact, all this was as nothing compared to the "work of the age" that was about to begin.

The Track Elevation Project

Until the development of local components of the interstate highway system following the passage of the National Interstate and Defense Highways Act in 1956, no single project had a greater impact on the physical form and urban character of downtown Indianapolis than the track elevation project. That undertaking's story was long and fractious, a complex interplay of transportation, business, and political interests—not to mention the concerns of the local citizenry—that resulted in a complete remaking of the Indianapolis Union Railway in a way that had a significant impact on the development patterns of the city. Its story could, and probably should, fill a book of its own.

The issue arose from the interplay of Indianapolis's streets and railroads. As was typical of many cities in the nineteenth century,[27] when the Hoosier capital's railroads were built they had to overlay their tracks on the existing street grid. Because they ran east–west, these rail lines had a negligible effect on the central city's east–west streets. Furthermore, for practical reasons having to do with cost and convenience, the railroads chose to locate south of the center of urban activity and development, thus causing minimal disruption of the city's heart. However, this meant that all the major north–south downtown streets ended up with railroad crossings at grade: Delaware, Pennsylvania, Meridian, Illinois, Tennessee (later Capitol Avenue), and Mississippi

(later Senate Avenue) streets all had crossings at grade and in a few years became further laced with yard tracks, industrial spurs, and multiple side tracks as freight traffic grew. Other crossings at East, Virginia, Missouri, and West streets meant a full mile—the east–west width of the original city plat—of daily train and street traffic conflicts.

At the time the 1853 Union Depot opened for business, the population of Indianapolis was small enough and railroad traffic light enough that the construction of tracks at grade to and through the city was of little import. Trains were not very frequent, they tended to be short, and pedestrian and vehicular traffic to and from the southern, less-developed part of town was fairly modest. At the time, it made sense to avoid the cost of building bridges or underpasses so that scarce capital could be devoted to construction of the railroad lines themselves. So street and railroad traffic met at grade crossings, with trains typically having the right of way, both legally and as a practical matter due to their size, speed, and inability to make quick stops. It did not take long, of course, for the grade crossing issue to get out of hand. As both Indianapolis and its railroad network grew in the third quarter of the nineteenth century, the conflict between street and rail traffic around Union Depot became more and more intolerable.

Interestingly, the track layout around the 1853 depot only aggravated the problem. Bypass tracks enabled freight trains, switching moves, light engines, and other traffic to avoid moving through the depot. But because the bypass tracks were on the north side of Union Depot, growing rail movements began to interfere with street traffic in the busy area between the depot and the Circle. Why the depot's planners made this choice has never been explained. Construction of the new Union Station in 1888 presented an opportunity to address the grade crossing problem, but the opportunity appears to have been largely lost. Yes, the tunnel in Illinois Street built in 1872 did provide a means for horse-drawn streetcars to pass under the Union Tracks; and yes, the 1888 depot project did enlarge and improve the tunnel; and yes, the bypass tracks were moved to the south side of the train shed; but none of this really solved the street/rail traffic problem. Photos from the era depict the situation quite dramatically. All of the new and enlarged track layout was still at grade, and worse yet, there were more tracks than ever before (in addition to the ten through and two stub station tracks, there were two or three more on the freight bypass). Since railroad traffic only promised to keep increasing, how, we can imagine the local citizenry asking, have the new depot and track layout improved things? The 1892 bridge that carried Virginia Avenue over the Union Tracks helped a little, but the street's angle to the southeast required anyone going to the area south and west of Union Station to double back several blocks. Of the other streets Meridian was the busiest, crossing the many tracks just east of the train shed. There had been discussions of whether to build a bridge on Meridian, but it never happened. Complete grade separation was the only logical answer, but it was a long time coming.

The "elevation" movement began with the city engineer's preparation of plans for the work, at the behest of the Common Council and apparently without much in the way of discussion with the affected railroads. An 1899 ordinance declared all at-grade trackage to be a nuisance and required that all tracks be elevated by September of 1901. The railroads dutifully ignored all of this, denying that the council had any authority to order such action, a position upheld by the state supreme court in 1903.[28] In 1905 the state legislature passed a law that enabled cities of more than 100,000 population (any guess as to how many Indiana cities of the period met that criterion?) to mandate grade separation of railroads, with the provision that the railroads in question pay 75 percent of the cost and the city and county 17 percent and 8 percent, respectively; a different formula applied when street railways were involved, but the steam railroad portion remained at 75 percent. The city's board of public works was to oversee all such projects.

Indianapolis lost no time, passing a 1905 council resolution requiring elevation of the tracks west of Capitol Avenue to a point west of West Street (Tennessee and Mississippi streets had been renamed Capitol and Senate avenues in the mid-1890s). This was an area about three blocks long that began at the west end of the Union Station train shed, so it affected all of the depot's approach tracks coming from the west, along with the Pullman Company coach yard west of Capitol and north of the tracks, and also numerous freight house and yard tracks. This work was completed, primarily by the Vandalia Road (Pennsylvania Railroad), in 1907. It involved some complicated engineering, grading, track relocation, and land acquisition, but it resulted in elevation of the tracks over Missouri Street and Kentucky Avenue at the point where those streets crossed each other, and over West Street. Capitol and Senate avenues were cut off by the elevation. The project placed the tracks some ten and a half feet above their original grade but fortunately required only a 1 percent grade (a one-foot

Figure 3.13 Although much of Union Station is blocked from view, the Union Station train shed's west end is quite visible. It has an ornamented cladding of glass and sheet metal, differentiating it from the open steel framework of the east end. To the left, on the shed's north side, is one of the two brick buildings that supported a smaller shed roof and also housed baggage facilities for the station.

Richard K. Baldwin collection

rise for every hundred feet of track) for trains moving westward from Union Station.[29]

Liking what it saw, the city passed an ordinance in 1907 that required elevation of all tracks east of Senate Avenue in the central area of Indianapolis. Unlike the earlier elevation work, which involved not only the Indianapolis Union Railway but also member railroads such as the Pennsylvania and the Big Four, this time the city was addressing only the IU, since all of the elevation work would involve only its tracks. Of course, the railroad share of costs would ultimately be paid by the IU's member roads. There

Figure 3.14 A scene from 1917 captures the Union Station train shed at a quiet hour. An eastbound local appears to be boarding passengers, but in the shed not much else is going on. On the right, however, to the south, the steel structure of the track elevation is well under way, so the old shed's days are numbered.

Richard K. Baldwin collection

was broad public support for the elevation, though there was also opposition. Some of that came from rail-served businesses facing the prospect of having to change their facilities to accommodate freight cars on industrial spurs that would be moved from ground level to the height of the elevated tracks. Photos from the era show that numerous businesses indeed had to do this, creating new doorways and loading docks at the second-floor level of their buildings.

The IU Railway dragged its feet like a child being taken to the woodshed, so the city kept hopefully passing additional elevation ordinances and resolutions. Finally the IU and the City of Indianapolis reached an agreement in June 1913, with a supplement in January 1915, specifying how the tracks and the train shed would be raised to the new elevation. The first work undertaken for the elevation project was the enclosing of Pogue's Run in a concrete twin box culvert. The poor old run was even then thought of as nothing but an open sewer, so underground it went; the part of it on IU property extended from Washington Street to Meridian Street. This did away with problems such as flooding and low, boggy ground.

SPECIAL INSTRUCTIONS.

1. The Indianapolis Union Railway Tracks are operated under the RULES GOVERNING EMPLOYES OF THE INDIANAPOLIS UNION RAILWAY COMPANY AND EMPLOYES OF OTHER COMPANIES WHEN USING BELT RAILROAD OR UNION TRACKS, EFFECTIVE FEBRUARY 1, 1910, and employes of all companies must provide themselves with a copy thereof before operating trains or engines on Union Tracks.

2. Trains or engines entering or leaving the Union Station must be governed by signals from the switch tenders, and must not pass fouling point of any track without first receiving proceed signal from switch tenders located to the east between Meridian and Pennsylvania streets, and to the west between west end of Union Station and Senate avenue.

3. Freight cuts must keep entirely out of the way of passenger trains, and must not occupy Union Tracks during hours prohibited by special instructions.

4. A man with proper signals must be stationed on the leading end of trains being backed, and in case of passenger trains must be provided with back-up hose for controlling trains, except in shifting or making up trains.

5. The engine bell must be rung continuously while trains or engines are moving.

6. Speed of trains over central passage-way in Union Station must not exceed three miles per hour. The passage-way must be opened promptly, or, when not practicable to do so, trainmen must, upon request from station employes, open vestibule doors.

7. Enginemen must so regulate their fires as to prevent engines from blowing off steam or causing unnecessary smoke while in or around the Station.

8. Conductors must see that closet doors of all cars are locked when trains are on Union Tracks.

9. Trainmen must, as far as practicable, not permit passengers to enter trains without first ascertaining that they have proper transportation, and for such points only as the train makes stops.

10. Conductors must, as far as practicable, ascertain whether baggage and mail for their trains has been loaded before leaving the Station.

11. Station officers and trainmen, when on duty, will direct passengers to their proper trains. Civil and gentlemanly deportment is required of all employes. Rudeness or incivility will not be tolerated. Employes must not enter into altercation with any person.

12. In case of an accident, names of witnesses must be taken and all facts reported promptly to the Superintendent.

P. J. LANDERS,
Superintendent.

INDIANAPOLIS UNION RAILWAY
Union Station
TIME TABLE
INDIANAPOLIS, IND.
No. 359.
SUNDAY, MAY 12, 1918.

Figures 3.15 and 3.16 (*Left and Facing*) The IU Railway for many years issued a timetable. The fact that number 359 was published as early as 1918 suggests how often the railroads adjusted their schedules. Only five railroad systems are listed because the New York Central controlled the Lake Erie & Western at that time. Special Instruction number 6 refers to the fact that the grade-level walkway from the station to the various tracks often was blocked by trains. Crews were required to keep the walkway open, but failing that, they would open car vestibules so people could climb up and then down, through the vestibules, to reach their proper tracks. Imagine how much fun that was with heavy luggage or long skirts. The new train shed, completed in 1922, would finally solve the problem.

Richard K. Baldwin collection

No. 359 On and after SUNDAY, MAY 12, 1918,   Trains will Run as follows—Central Standard Time:

NEW YORK CENTRAL LINES.
(BIG FOUR ROUTE.)

DEPART. — **ARRIVE.**

CLEVELAND DIVISION.

DEPART	ARRIVE
24 American Ex., dy.no pas.. 3.20am	43 Southwestern Mail, s.dy..12.15am
46 N.Y.&NewEng.Sp.,d.s.dy. 7.00am	5 Buff-Det-St.L.Ex., d.s.dy.. 7.45am
46 Elkhart-Benton Harb. Ex. 7.00am	39 Lake Special, dy.........12.00noon
10 Cleveland Accom. †.........10.00am	41 Southwestern Mail, dy.....11.40am
40 Lake Special, p.dy.......... 5.40pm	11 S'thwes'n Lm., cl.d.s.dy...11.50am
18 Knick'bocker Spl.,d.s.dy. 6.15pm	33 Clev.-Ind'polis Sp., dy..... 7.30pm
2 Detroit & Toledo Ex.,s.dy 9.00pm	33 Benton Harb.-Elkhart Ex. 7.30pm
20 N.Y. Cen. Lim., cl.s.dy.....11.45pm	

ST. LOUIS DIVISION.

DEPART	ARRIVE
48 Southwestern Mail, s.dy..12.30am	24 American Ex., no pass. dy 2.45am
5 Buffalo-St.L.Ex., cl.s.d.dy 7.55am	46 N.Y.& New Eng.Lim.,s.dy 5.00am
11 So'wes'n Lim.,cl.d.s.dy.12.00noon	2 Mat. & Terre Haute Acc.†.10.30am
41 Southwertern Mail, p.dy.12.10pm	16 St. Louis-Cin. Sp., p.d.dy. 2.40pm
3 Terre Haute & Mat. Acc. † 4.15pm	18 Knick'bocker Spl., d.s.dy 6.05pm
	20 N.Y. Cen. Lim., cl.d.s.dy.11.40pm

CINCINNATI DIVISION.

DEPART	ARRIVE
34 Night Express, dy............ 3.40am	43 St.L.& Chi. Night Ex.,dy..12.15am
46 Cincin. Night Sp., d.s.dy.. 5.10am	35 Chicago Night Sp., s.dy... 2.35am
36 Cincinnati Express, p.dy.. 7.30am	1 Cincinnati Accom. †.........10.20am
10 Queen City Lm., d.p.dy.12.00noon	29 Cincinnati Acc.Sun.only.11.00am
10 Louisville Special, b.dy.12.00noon	15 Chic. & St. L. Ex., d.p.dy.11.50am
16 Cincinnati Ex., d.dy..... 2.55pm	19 White City Spl., p.d.dy 2.35pm
14 Cincinnati Accom., dy.... 3.30pm	27 Cincinnati Express, p.dy.. 6.20pm
18 Queen City Spec.,d.p.s.dy 6.15pm	27 Louisville Special, dy..... 6.20pm
	33 Pivot City Lim., d.p.dy.. 8.45pm

CHICAGO DIVISION.

DEPART	ARRIVE
43 Chicago Night Ex., dy.....12.30am	34 Night Express, s.dy......... 3.10am
35 Chicago Night Spl., s. dy.. 2.45am	46 Cincin. Night Sp., s.dy..... 5.00am
9 Kankakee & Chicago Ac.† 6.00am	2 Kankakee Accom. †.........10.50am
15 Chicago Ex., d.p.dy.s.12.00noon	16 Cincinnati Ex., d.dy..... 2.40pm
19 White City Spl., d.p.dy..... 2.40pm	18 Queen City Spec.,p.d.dy. 6.05pm

MICHIGAN DIVISION.

DEPART	ARRIVE
40 Lake Special, bb.dy......... 5.40pm	39 Elkhart Express, bb.dy..12.00noon

PEORIA DIVISION.

DEPART	ARRIVE
43 Peoria Express, s.dy.........12.25am	44 Columbus & Cin.Ex.,s.dy. 3.10am
9 Peoria Ex. and Mail †...... 7.00am	16 New York & Ohio Spl.,†... 2.50pm
11 Western Exp., p.b.dy.......11.55am	18 Peoria Express, p.b.dy...... 6.00pm

SPRINGFIELD (O.) DIVISION.

DEPART	ARRIVE
30 Chic. & Colum. Spl., s.dy.. 3.20am	31 Colum. & Chic. Spl., s.dy.. 2.30am
16 Col. & Springfield Ex.†... 3.10pm	15 Columbus Express †.........11.50am

LAKE ERIE & WESTERN R. R.

DEPART	ARRIVE
20 Mich. City & S.B'd Ex., †... 7.00am	23 Indianapolis Spl, bb.dy... 1.50pm
24 South Bend Spl., bb.dy... 5.15pm	25 Mich. City & S.B'd Ex. †..... 9.45pm

ILLINOIS CENTRAL R. R.

DEPART	ARRIVE
301 New Orleans Ex., dy....... 6.40am	304 Indianapolis Ex., dy.......11.15am
303 New Orleans Passeng., dy. 5.00pm	302 Indianapolis Passeng., dy. 8.45pm

---

PENNSYLVANIA LINES.
(P., C., C. & ST. L. R. R.)

DEPART. — **ARRIVE.**

INDIANAPOLIS DIVISION.

DEPART	ARRIVE
114 Eastern Mail, s.dy........... 4.05am	113 St. Louis & Chic. Ex., s.dy 2.15am
802 Columbus Accom., dy..... 7.05am	13 Mail and Ex., no pass. †... 2.45am
72 St.L.-Pitt.-N.Y.Ex., s.d.dy 7.45am	27 The Commerc'l Ex.,d.s.dy 6.45am
20 Keystone Ex., s.d.dy....... 3.00pm	21 Keystone Ex., s.d.dy.......10.55am
108 Eastern Express, dy......... 4.40pm	803 Indianapolis Acc., dy.......12.01pm
*x30 The New Yorker,s.l.d.dy 5.45pm	*x31 The St. Louisan,s.l.d.dy12.10pm
26 Commercial Ex., s.d.dy.... 6.45pm	71 N.Y.-Pitts.-St. L. Ex., dy... 3.15pm
144 Pittsburgh Ex., s.dy.........10.10pm	11 St. Louis Mail, no pas., dy 8.04pm
	135 Indianapolis Acc., s.dy.....11.35pm

CHICAGO DIVISION.

DEPART	ARRIVE
307 Midnight Express, s.dy.... 1.55am	336 Louisville Night Ex., s.dy 3.50am
317 Chic. Daylight Ex.,p.b.dy.11.30am	316 Lou. Daylight Ex., p.b.dy. 3.05pm

LOUISVILLE DIVISION.

DEPART	ARRIVE
336 Louisville Night Ex.,s.dy. 4.05am	307 Midnight Express, s.dy..... 1.45am
326 Lou. & Mad. F.L., s.bb.dy.. 7.45am	917 Madison Accom., dy.........10.25am
316 Lou. & Mad. Ex., b.p.dy.. 3.20pm	317 Chic. Daylight Ex. p.b.dy.11.20am
916 Madison Accom., dy....... 5.00pm	827 Louisville Accom., dy....... 2.30pm
846 Louisville Accom., dy..... 7.10pm	847 Lou. & Mad. Acc., bb.dy... 6.10pm
	327 Lou. & Pitt. F.L., dy...... 9.50pm

ST. LOUIS DIVISION.

DEPART	ARRIVE
113 St. L. & Chic. Ex., b.s.dy.. 2.20am	114 Eastern Mail, s.dy........... 3.50am
13 Mail and Ex., no pass. †... 2.55am	72 St.L.-Pitts.-N.Y.Ex., s.dy.. 7.30am
27 The Commerc'l Ex., d.s.dy 7.00am	806 Indianapolis Special, dy...10.00am
21 Keystone Ex., p.d.s.dy.....11.00am	20 Keystone Ex., s.d.dy......... 2.50pm
*31 The St. Louisan, s.l.d.dy.12.17pm	108 Eastern Express, dy.......... 4.10pm
71 N.Y.-Pitts.-St.L.Ex., s.dy.. 3.20pm	*x30 The New Yorker,s.l.d.dy. 5.40pm
837 T.H. and Eff'ham Sp., dy 4.40pm	26 Commercial Ex., s.d.dy..... 6.35pm
11 The St. Louis Mail, dy...... 8.16pm	144 Pittsburgh Ex., b.s.dy.......10.00pm
135 Western Express, dy.......11.50pm	

VINCENNES DIVISION.

DEPART	ARRIVE
407 Fr. Lick & Vinc. Ex., p.dy 8.00am	406 Vin. & Fr. Lick Ex., p.dy.10.30am
487 Fr. Lick & Vinc. Ex., p.dy 4.50pm	426 Vin. & Fr. Lick Ex., p.dy. 6.15pm

CHICAGO, IND'PLS & LOU. R'Y (MONON ROUTE.)

DEPART	ARRIVE
36 Chi. Night Express, s.dy ... 1.35am	35 Cincinnati Vestibule, s.dy 5.00am
32 The Hoosier, d.p.dy......... 7.45am	17 Monon Accom., dy.........10.30am
38 Cin. & Chic. Ex., p.d.dy.12.00noon	37 Chi. & Cin. Exp., p.d.dy... 2.20pm
30 Cin. & Chic. Lim., p.dy... 4.00pm	33 Chic. & Cin. Lim., d.p.dy 3.50pm
18 Monon Accom., dy......... 5.30pm	31 The Hoosier, p.d.dy.........10.30pm

CINCINNATI, INDIANAPOLIS & WESTERN R. R.
CINCINNATI DIVISION.

DEPART	ARRIVE
35 Cincinnati Vestibule, s.dy 5.10am	36 Cincinnati Vest., s.dy....... 1.20am
31 Cin. Tol. & Det.Ex.d.p.dy.10.30am	38 Cin. & Chic. Ex., p.dy.......11.50am
37 Cinc. & Dayton Ex., p.dy.. 2.55pm	30 Cin. & Chi. Lim., d.p.dy... 3.50pm
33 Chi. & Cin. Lim.,d.p.dy.... 5.25pm	32 Cin. & Ind'pls Ex., p.d.dy 8.10pm

SPRINGFIELD (ILL.) DIVISION.

DEPART	ARRIVE
10 Springfield Mail and Ex. † 6.30am	11 Springfield Accom. †.........12.15pm
12 Springfield Acc., p.b. †..... 4.00pm	13 Springf'd Mail & Ex., p.b.† 9.45pm

---

For the government and information of employes only. The Company reserves the right to vary therefrom as circumstances may require.

TRAINS MARKED THUS		
dy.—Daily.	p.—Parlor Car.	d.—Dining Car.	l.—Library-Smoking Car.	¶—Daily Except Monday.
s.—Sleeper.	c.—Chair Car.	b.—Buffet Car.	bl.—Buffet-Library Car.	†—Daily Except Sunday.
*—No Coach Passengers.	cl.—Club Car.	bb.—Broiler-Buffet Car.	x.—Extra Fare.	‡—Daily Except Tuesday.

Figure 3.17 (*Above*) In May 1919 nearly all of the original Union Station train shed is gone. This view looks west from the shed's east end, just off South Meridian Street. Out of view to the left, several of the new elevated platforms of the new train shed are already in use, and within three years the entire track elevation and train shed will be complete.

Richard K. Baldwin collection

Figure 3.18 (*Facing*) An eastward view toward Union Station, dating from around 1920, shows that all the original ground-level tracks have been torn up and some new elevated platforms are in use. Those closest to the station have not yet been built, and work on the new train shed is just getting under way. The Illinois Central's connection to the track elevation curves in from the right.

Indiana Historical Society, Bass Photo Co. Collection

Figure 3.19 Wet platforms in the Union Station train shed suggest that during the construction period getting to and from one's train could be unpleasant. The steel structure appears to be done, but the concrete roof structure is not. The view is westward, with tracks 11 and 10 in the foreground.

Indiana Historical Society, Bass Photo Co. Collection

Figure 3.20 Compare this view, circa 1922, to the earlier one in figure 3.18. The train shed is complete, and soot marks on the entry arches show that all the tracks are in use. There actually are thirteen of them, but the one farthest to the left is a stub track that ends within the train shed. Track 12, on the right, has a roof supported by posts along its outer edge. This track and most of its roof were later removed, probably to make room for easing the sharp curvature of the adjacent freight bypass tracks.

Indiana Historical Society, Bass Photo Co. Collection

Figure 3.21 A 1924 westward view from the connection to the Pennsylvania Railroad's Louisville line shows the train shed and head house of Union Station. The open gallery-like structure of the south side of the shed is visible. Today a steel-framed sheet metal enclosure along this side of the shed reduces the visual effect of passing freight trains.

Indiana Historical Society, Bass Photo Co. Collection

Figure 3.22 Taken about the time the train shed was completed in 1922, this photo shows the steel framework, concrete roof structure with smoke slots, and the skylights that made the new train shed a much more pleasant place than the old one.

Indiana Historical Society, Bass Photo Co. Collection

Figure 3.23 The concourse of the new train shed was much nicer, too. Protected from weather, wind, and locomotive smoke, passengers used well-marked doorways and stairs up to the various platforms and spent minimal time outdoors before boarding. This concourse was at the original level of the old train shed's platforms and had finishes of painted concrete and polychrome terra-cotta in light colors.

Indiana Historical Society, Bass Photo Co. Collection

Figure 3.24 Wintertime of 1929 finds Union Station as busy as ever. Compare this view to earlier ones. Horse-drawn vehicles no longer grace the streets, and the north approach to the Illinois Street tunnel has been filled in due to conversion of the tunnel to a passageway for baggage trucks serving the station's platforms.

Indiana Historical Society,
Bass Photo Co. Collection

Next came construction of retaining walls, bridge abutments, and pedestals for the columns that would support the elevation under the new train shed, along with the conversion of the Illinois Street tunnel into a baggage tunnel. The retaining wall along the south side of the project was located far enough south so that four additional through tracks could be added to the eight tracks under the existing train shed, along with the freight bypass tracks. This was followed by construction of bridges and other structural elements of the elevation, along with reworking of some of the approach tracks. All of this was done without significant changes to the existing tracks or disruption of train service. The first four new elevated tracks (those located farthest south) were placed in service on August 1, 1918; this required some extra walking and stair climbing for passengers in order to reach the newly elevated tracks, but the railroads still provided full service. Then came demolition of the original train shed and abandonment and removal of the four outermost (southernmost) existing tracks under the shed. The four new elevated tracks that replaced them went into service early in 1919, followed by the final four northernmost tracks and a new single stub track on the north side, in the western half of the new train shed. (As a result, period photos show thirteen tracks at the west end of the shed but only twelve at the east end.)

Those last-built tracks remained in service while work began on the new low-roof train shed. Measuring 930 by 250 feet, it was a huge structure resting entirely on a system of steel beams and columns (540 of the latter) so that in this area the 22-foot-high elevation would have usable open space beneath the shed. The shed had components on three levels: below grade was the baggage tunnel in the old Illinois Street tunnel; at grade or street level was the new 104-foot-wide passenger concourse that extended from the depot building to the south side of the elevation, flanked on east and west by baggage, mail, express, and mechanical spaces extending the entire length and width of the train shed; and at the new elevated track level were the twelve passenger tracks, platforms, and platform roofs, along with the one stub track on the north side and the freight bypass tracks south of track 12. The entire shed was built in two parts, with the portion over the southernmost seven tracks the first to be done; it was in service for some time before elevation of the final tracks and completion of the shed. Built of structural steel and cast-in-place concrete, the train shed had east and west exterior walls with arched openings for the tracks. These walls were finished in light-colored brick with terra-cotta trim that included the track number above each track. Track 12 was only partially covered, in a manner suggesting that the designers intended to make it possible to enlarge the shed if traffic warranted.

All manner of facts and statistics convey the scale of the track elevation project. Its final cost was just under $10 million. The brick-clad east wing office building at the train shed's northeast corner was three stories high and measured 25 by 200 feet; the Pullman Company coach yard west and north of the shed had eight tracks holding thirty-eight cars; the elevation eliminated fourteen grade crossings and the Virginia Avenue bridge; additional land beyond already-existing railroad land acquired for the project totaled 458,000 square feet, some ten and a half acres; and more than 465,000 cubic yards of fill material went into the embankments that raised the tracks to the new level (had it been piled into a column three feet on a side, it would have been almost ten miles high).

In architectural design, the new train shed and the concourse below it were distinctly different from the Union Station of 1888, a reflection of changing tastes as the late nineteenth century turned into the early twentieth. The shed's east and west ends, which had limited ornamentation and stylistic treatment, contrasted in their light colors and simple design with the dark and heavily ornamented exterior of the depot building. In the interior the differences were even more distinct. The depot's interior design was firmly late Victorian in character, employing classically inspired space and design elements, richly ornamented and with a somewhat ponderous feel; it was fairly dark as well. In contrast, the concourse, which was reached through doorways in the south wall of the depot's first floor, had a skylight at the point where it joined the depot, and its surfaces—columns, walls, and the enclosures of the arrival and departure stairways connecting the concourse to the platforms—all were finished in polychrome terra-cotta glazed in light shades of cream, green, and earth tones.

The terrazzo floor was light colored, as were the painted plaster ceilings.

These distinctions, however, paled in importance when one took a larger view of the elevation project. It had delivered to Indianapolis a modern transportation facility, properly sized to the traffic it had to serve, and employing all of the best practices of the time: abundant trackage to speed the comings and goings of the trains, modern signaling and communications systems to make operations more efficient, separate arrival and departure stairs to speed up boarding and detraining, and safe and comfortable pathways from street to trainside. For the city at large, the track elevation project eliminated the most vexatious problem posed by the existence of so much rail traffic so close to the heart of Indianapolis: the grade crossings were gone. No longer would pedestrians and vehicles suffer delays while locomotives and trains trundled back and forth. The numerous underpasses on all the major streets crossed by the tracks of the Indianapolis Union Railway made it seem almost as if the railroad were not even there.

In February 1916 the Coburn Photo and Film Company of Indianapolis sent employee H. P. Heald to photograph the Indianapolis Union Railway before the track elevation project started. He took at least thirty-two photos over two days, most likely with a bulky 8x10 view camera, judging from a few instances where his and the camera's shadows appear in a photo. Six years later, Heald returned to the same locations for "after" photos showing the completed work. The result is a remarkable visual record of a project that changed the face of downtown Indianapolis, the effects of which are still felt today. On the following pages, five pairs of these views (with 1916 on the left pages and 1922 on the right) provide a sense of how dramatic the change was.

Figure 3.25 Looking south on Illinois Street, Union Station is on the left and commercial buildings on the right, including the Spencer House hotel. Ahead is the original train shed, which could be entered from Illinois Street and beneath which runs the tunnel that separated streetcar and rail traffic but left precious little room for any adventurous pedestrians.

Brian Banta Collection

Figure 3.26 By 1922, with completion of the track elevation, Illinois Street still has a tunnel, but it is no longer accessible from the street. The old approach ramps have been filled in, and the part under the train shed is now a baggage tunnel, with elevators to the platforms. Illinois Street is tidier, now partially smooth-paved rather than paved with the rougher paving stones of earlier days, and the Spencer House sign and entry canopy have been altered.

Brian Banta Collection

Figure 3.27 Inside Union Station's original train shed, this was the 1916 view looking north from the walkway (also called the midway or passageway; see Special Instruction number 6, shown in figure 3.15) that led from the station across the tracks. Note the large signs with track numbers oriented so people coming from the station could read them.

Brian Banta Collection

Figure 3.28 The newly completed train shed made life much easier for passengers, since the need to walk across active tracks had been eliminated. Next to the tree-like roof column, brakeman's lanterns, marker lamps, and a flag await the call to duty.

Brian Banta Collection

Figure 3.29 In a view looking southwest from the corner of Meridian and Louisiana streets in 1916, we get a good view of the eastern baggage building and the east end of the original train shed. An early flivver idles at the curb, and an eastbound New York Central train is standing in the shed.

Brian Banta Collection

Figure 3.30 Six years later, the track elevation and new train shed have completely altered the scene. Auto design has evolved further, and the hotel on the corner has changed its name; this building is still standing.

Brian Banta Collection

Figure 3.31 At the train shed's west end in 1916 there is more activity than at the east end because there are several spur tracks for baggage, mail, and express cars. Some baggage carts are loaded with milk cans, once a sizable business on the railroads. Tracks in the foreground are the leads to the Indianapolis Street Railway Company's Louisiana Street carbarn. Above the baggage car at the right, the shed's exposed structure indicates that demolition has begun.

Brian Banta Collection

Figure 3.32 The rebuilt train shed completely changed the scene from six years earlier. This portion of the station facilities handled baggage and express. Note the express wagon horses standing in the recessed dock doorways; one of them has left his calling card on the street railway tracks. Streetcars would disappear from Indianapolis in 1953.

Brian Banta Collection

Figure 3.33 Locomotive steam and smoke obscure Union Station's original train shed, at center between the two large buildings. Delaware Street is in the foreground of this 1916 westward view; the eastern connection to the Pennsylvania Railroad's Louisville line veers off to the left.

Brian Banta Collection

Figure 3.34 In 1922 the photographer was up on the new track elevation just east of the bridge over Delaware Street. Tracks to Louisville turn to the left; the new train shed is faintly visible beyond the new second-story loading dock built by the Indiana Refrigerating Company in order to retain rail service. As in the 1916 photo, all switches here are manually operated, but this would change with the 1931 completion of IU tower and the interlocking plant controlling east end trackage.

Brian Banta Collection

Figure 3.35 (*Above*) As part of the track elevation project, the Pennsylvania Railroad built its produce yard east of Union Station. This photo, dating from the 1920s, looks southeast from the intersection of Delaware Street and Virginia Avenue. Although the yard is gone, the "Pennsylvania Lines" lettering and PRR keystone at the bottom of the truck ramp have been preserved at the Indiana Transportation Museum. The Big Four also had an elevated yard east of the Pennsylvania's.

Indiana Historical Society, P0383

Figure 3.36 (*Facing*) Another high-level view looking south toward Union Station, probably taken in the late 1940s or early 1950s, shows that the canopy on the Jackson Place entry has been replaced with the "streamlined" one that remains in place today. The fountains in Jackson Place have been removed to facilitate arrivals and departures by automobile. South of the train shed, commercial development has surged, although most of the buildings in this view would be demolished over the next few decades.

Indiana Historical Society, Bass Photo Co. Collection

Figure 3.37 (*Facing*) A quiet interlude at Union Station in the 1940s finds redcaps helping passengers with their luggage. The ticket office that was installed in the Grand Hall in 1913 has been moved elsewhere (its footprint is faintly visible in the floor), leaving the central hall unobstructed again. Beyond the south doorway, just inside the 1922 concourse, is the information desk with its arrival and departure boards.

Indiana Historical Society, Bass Photo Co. Collection

Figure 3.38 (*Right*) Taken in the 1950s, this view looks north toward the Jackson Place entry doors of Union Station. The building had been in service for over a half century by this time and had endured many alterations (note the luggage lockers once found in almost every transportation center), but its original character remained largely intact.

Gene Maresca collection

Figure 3.39 In the 1950s the northwest portion of the Grand Hall gained a new ticket counter. Impressively automated for its time, its zigzag counters and clumsy suspended fluorescent lights showed little respect for the character of the historic station. Compare this to the similar view in figure 3.38.

John Fuller collection

Figure 3.40 It is wartime in Indianapolis (the strolling couple is passing a pair of recruiting posters), and Union Station is experiencing unprecedented travel demand. The ornate entry canopy would be replaced several years later by the more modern one visible in figure 3.36.

Bob's Photos, Jay Williams collection

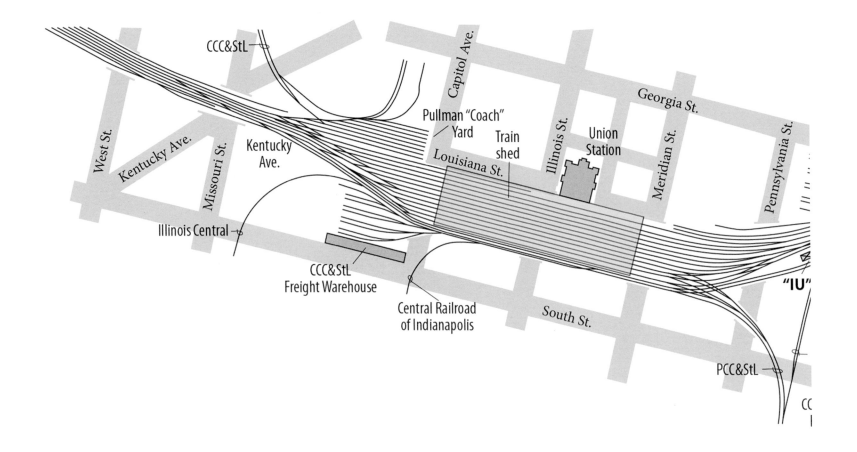

Map 3.1 This map is redrawn from a track plan issued by the Indianapolis Union Railway. By the spring of 1922 the Union (the downtown trackage, not including the leased Belt Railroad) had pretty well reached its greatest extent. The new Union Station train shed and the massive track elevation were complete, and several of the participating railroads still had major downtown freight facilities. Curving across South Street, the Central Railroad of Indianapolis was a local switching road dating from 1899 and long under the control of the Big Four. Remember that this was before the reconstruction of tracks east of the train shed and the opening of the new IU Tower in 1931; prior to that improvement, the whole maze of east end switches shown here was entirely hand-operated by an army of switch tenders.

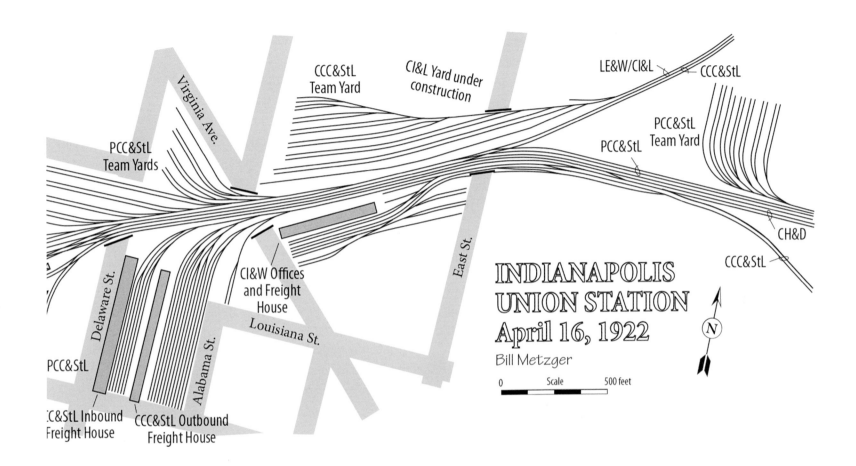

PCC&StL
Team Yards

CCC&StL
Team Yard

CI&L Yard under
construction

LE&W/CI&L

CCC&StL

Virginia Ave.

PCC&StL

PCC&StL
Team Yard

CH&D

CCC&StL

CI&W Offices
and Freight
House

East St.

Delaware St.

Louisiana St.

Alabama St.

PCC&StL

CC&StL Inbound
Freight House

CCC&StL Outbound
Freight House

INDIANAPOLIS
UNION STATION
April 16, 1922

Bill Metzger

0   Scale   500 feet

N

111

TRACK IMPROVEMENTS

It turned out, however, that the IU Railway was not quite done with improvements. A major undertaking that followed shortly on the work completed between 1913 and 1922 came in 1931, when the Union Switch & Signal Company (US&S) of Swissvale, Pennsylvania, finished a thorough rebuilding of the approach tracks at the east end of the train shed. Full operation began on June 16 of that year. Included were all station tracks, the freight bypass tracks, the wye connection to the Pennsylvania Railroad's Louisville line, and the tracks that diverged into the various railroads' lines to the east. It also included construction of IU Tower to oversee all the east end tracks and serve as the heart of the all-new interlocking plant.[30] The project was documented in a promotional booklet published by US&S, which in turn was a reprint of an article in the August 1931 issue of *Railway Signaling*.[31] This interlocking plant would serve Union Station for more than eight decades; today, at least for now, IU Tower still stands, and the ghost of the 1931 project can still be seen in the sparse (though quite active) trackage that remains in place.

As told by US&S, the story began with the outdated train routing system still in place in the late 1920s: "The previous method of handling and routing the heavy traffic through the terminal was by means of mechanical signals and switches operated on the ground by approximately 13 men on each trick [working shift] in the eastern half of the terminal alone. This method proved inadequate and unsatisfactory, and, in order to secure the desired safety and speed of manipulation for the numerous passenger train and switch engine movements, an intensive study of the requirements was undertaken."[32]

The booklet noted that Union Station had an average of 200 train movements daily; over 24 hours that meant a movement every 7.2 minutes, and at peak times the headway surely was much briefer; that must have kept the switch tenders really hopping. All this was swept away when the new tower was completed and the new track arrangement entered service. Once that occurred, only one or two tower operators, who had complete control of switches and signals, could handle all of the movements that passed by the east end of Union Station. Oddly enough, however, similar improvements were planned but never undertaken at the west end of the station. It is possible that this was due to financial constraints during the Depression; and that heavy traffic during World War II precluded taking west end trackage out of service long enough to install an interlocking plant. Then, in the postwar years, declining traffic levels likely made such an expenditure unnecessary. In any case, operations at the west throat of Union Station would remain manual. West of the throat, the Peoria & Eastern, the Baltimore & Ohio, the New York Central, and the Pennsylvania all diverged onto their separate routes, and farther west, all of them crossed the Indianapolis Belt Railroad at grade. And that railroad, which was freight-only and well outside downtown Indianapolis, had its own intriguing story of nineteenth-century railroad innovation.

Figure 3.41 In a westward view from IU Tower, one of the Pennsylvania Railroad's legendary T1 Duplexes drifts by, while several of the diesels that ultimately would displace steam idle in the background. The photo is undated, but likely is from the early 1950s. The T1 was known for being "slippery" but on the straightaways of the Midwest nothing could catch it.

R. A. Frederick photo, Jay Williams collection

Figure 3.42 Baltimore & Ohio's number 5199, a Pacific, heads west out of Union Station in 1947 with a very modest two-car train, bound for Illinois. The station still hosted a robust roster of Pennsylvania and New York Central trains in the immediate postwar era, but the more minor railroads of Indianapolis were able to offer less and less service.

Bob's Photos, Jay Williams collection

Figure 3.43 Rolling east near IU Tower, the Monon's westbound *Hoosier* (which had to leave Union Station headed east) has just begun its journey to Chicago. The photo is undated but likely was made in the late 1940s.

John Holliday photo, Jay Williams collection

Figure 3.44 (*Facing*) The New York Central and the Pennsylvania were the "big dogs" of Indianapolis railroading. With the downtown skyline as a backdrop, NYC Mohawk number 3139 is ready to wheel an eastbound over the former Big Four around 1951.

Hal Lewis photo, Jay Williams collection

Figure 3.45 (*Right*) NYC E-7 Lightning-striped A and B units on the westbound *Knickerbocker* are passing Kentucky Avenue, having just left Union Station on their run to St. Louis. The 12-car train is a mix of heavyweight cars and lightweights of the Great Steel Fleet. A guess as to the date would be the mid-1950s, when this train carried sleeping cars to St. Louis from Boston, New York, Buffalo, Cleveland, and Detroit, as well as one from Detroit to Indianapolis.

Bob Lorenz photo, Jay Williams collection

Figure 3.46 The good times could not last, not for the New York Central, not for the Pennsylvania, not for anyone else. The PRR had its own roster of name trains: *Spirit of St. Louis* and *Penn Texas* between New York and St. Louis; *Southland* and *South Wind* between Chicago and Louisville on the way to Florida, along with many others. This photo is undated and the train name is not noted, but excessive weeds, simplified paint schemes, and unwashed equipment suggest that the sun is setting rapidly on the passenger train.

Mont Switzer photo

NOTES

1. Holloway, *Indianapolis*, 81; punctuation and capitalization in original. The *Hanna*, it will be recalled, was the steamboat that in 1831 so miserably failed to prove the navigability—or so successfully proved the non-navigability—of the White River.

2. This situation in itself presented a new business opportunity: the transfer of passengers and their baggage between terminals. Owners of cabs, hacks, drays, and buggies quickly responded to this form of economic stimulus. Those of a certain age will remember the fleet of Parmelee Transfer Company limousines, with smartly uniformed drivers, that connected all of Chicago's downtown depots until the Amtrak era and survives today as the Continental Airport Express bus service.

3. Richard S. Simons and Francis H. Parker, *Railroads of Indiana* (Bloomington: Indiana University Press, 1997), 14–15. The former Bellefontaine or

Big Four line, today operated by CSX Transportation, still carries considerable traffic over the curves, grade crossings, and street overpasses of this somewhat circuitous route. A plan from the Penn Central era would have rerouted this line over a portion of the east leg of the Indianapolis Belt and to the Pennsylvania Railroad's Pan Handle route on the city's east side, but this never went forward.

4. Rybczynski, *Clearing in the Distance*, 329.

5. Indianapolis development patterns map, Indiana State Library.

6. Indianapolis city map, Indiana State Library.

7. James R. Hetherington, *Indianapolis Union Station* (Carmel, IN: Guild Press of Indiana, 2000), 5.

8. Ibid., 5.

9. Wesley Shank, *Union Station: Written Historical and Descriptive Data* (Washington, DC: Historic American Buildings Survey, National Park Service, HABS No. IND-65, August 1971), 5.

10. This railroad was soon renamed the Indianapolis & Cincinnati.

11. This passage is from a photocopy. It did not include a source citation but is very likely from one of a series of corporate histories of the Pennsylvania Railroad and affiliated railroad companies published in the 1940s in connection with the PRR's centennial. Holdings of land and tracks that had remained with the proprietary companies were transferred to the Indianapolis Union Railway Company in March of 1884.

12. Shank, *Union Station*, 5.

13. Ibid., 5–6.

14. John H. White, quoted in James R. Hetherington, "The History of Union Station," paper presented at the 2003 Railroad Symposium, Indiana Historical Society, archived at www.indianahistory.org, unpaginated.

15. Railway and Locomotive Historical Society. *Railroad History*, no. 137, 37.

16. Hetherington, "History of Union Station."

17. *I.U. Ry. Co. Report of Original Cost*. Undated carbon copy of typescript in the collections of the William Henry Smith Memorial Library, Indiana Historical Society. This report uses particular terminology and is worded in a way that makes it almost certain it was produced as part of the ICC-mandated valuation effort. It likely dates from late 1922 or sometime in 1923.

18. Hetherington, "History of Union Station," n.p.

19. Ibid.

20. Bodenhamer and Barrows, *Encyclopedia of Indianapolis*, 838.

21. The standard reference on this subject remains Carroll Meeks's seminal work: Carroll L. V. Meeks, *The Railroad Station* (New Haven, CT: Yale University Press, 1956).

22. The umbrella shed consisted of a line of posts or columns along a platform, with a gable roof located clear of passing train cars; gutters at the roof edge were necessary to keep rainwater from dripping onto passengers. The butterfly shed inverted the gable, giving the roof a Y shape and employing downspouts along the column line to carry water to underground drain lines. The Bush shed was a form of butterfly shed in which each platform roof connected to the next and had a central slot to remove locomotive exhaust.

23. John A. Droege, *Passenger Terminals and Trains* (New York: McGraw-Hill Book Company, 1916); facsimile reprint by Kalmbach Publishing Company, 1969, 10–11, 40–42.

24. Shank, *Union Station*, 1–6.

25. "Organized Movement Demanded," Indianapolis *Sun*, February 18, 1910, n.p.

26. Letter, Indianapolis Union Railway to Indianapolis Chamber of Commerce, June 3, 1913. Collection of Brian Banta.

27. See, for instance, Rybczynski, *Clearing in the Distance*.

28. Most facts about the track elevation project are drawn from the *I.U. Ry. Co. Report of Original Cost*, cited in note 17.

29. *The Railroad Gazette* 43, no. 26 (December 27, 1907): 774–8.

30. "Interlocking" refers to the fact that such facilities were designed so that the setting of the track switches and associated signals for a particular movement through defined limits were "interlocked" in such a way that the signals could not give false indications, and so that conflicting movements could not be set up.

31. *The Indianapolis Terminal, Bulletin No. 149* (Swissvale, PA: Union Switch & Signal Co., May 1932). Copy from collection of Richard K. Baldwin.

32. Ibid., n.p.

4

THE BELT:
ANOTHER NEW IDEA

THE UNION TRACKS built as part of the Union Depot project carried passenger and freight trains as well as local switching moves; in the early years they were more than adequate for the traffic they carried. The tracks enabled interchange of cars between railroads, and for shipments originating or terminating in downtown Indianapolis the railroads built freight houses and spur tracks.[1] It would not be long, however, before the Union Tracks became too crowded.

The pioneer Madison & Indianapolis (M&I) built its depot on the south side of South Street between Pennsylvania and Delaware streets, now a vacant lot with some surviving stone retaining walls. By June of 1850 the M&I was connected to the Union Tracks by a wye track whose successor remains in place today. A surge of railroad building followed, and by 1870 Indianapolis was celebrated as "the Railroad City." A map published that year shows clearly that the downtown was already a complex ganglion of radiating railroad lines and numerous sidings and spur tracks.[2] By the end of the nineteenth century, fourteen of the sixteen rail lines that would serve the city were in place—the

final two opened in 1906 and 1918—and nearly every railroad aimed directly for the narrow downtown corridor formed by the Union Tracks.

This unavoidably led to the need for a specialized type of railroad. The line-haul part of carrying freight was always fairly simple: put a car in a train going in the right direction. What happened before and after the line-haul, though, was more complex: gathering and sorting cars and assembling them into trains, often in a particular order; switching them onto one or more connecting railroads; and sorting out and delivering them to a final destination. As the rail network and customer base grew ever larger, efficient interchange—the transfer of freight cars among different railroads—was critical and became a real logistical challenge. This gave birth to belt lines (which were also called terminal, switching, or connecting railroads), often subsidiaries or joint ventures of line-haul roads, with the purpose of speeding interchange between railroads and picking up and delivering freight cars to customers on the belt lines. These specialized railroads kept much originating, terminating, and local freight traffic off the line-haul railroads' main routes through a city, improving traffic flow overall. Most dated from the late nineteenth and early twentieth century and could be found in places such as Houston, New Orleans, Chicago, and even Hannibal, Missouri. Chicago's Elgin, Joliet & Eastern Railway, the "Chicago Outer Belt," was among the largest at 238 route miles and nearly 1,100 total miles of track.[3] The Association of American Railroads recorded some 210 "terminal and switching companies" as of 1947.[4]

In the Indianapolis of the 1870s, dense rail traffic in the Union Tracks corridor caused confusion and delays. Maps of the era show many spur tracks and freight houses, not to mention engine terminals and railroad shop buildings, that impeded the flow of freight traffic. But it turned out that cattle, sheep, and hogs, of all things, inspired the belt railroad that would solve the problem.

The packing business of Indianapolis was just beginning its great development. Kingan & Company had moved their plant to Indianapolis from Cincinnati . . . and opened on November 16th, 1863. . . . They erected in 1870 a small stock yards [*sic*] near their plant. For a while the Kingan yards answered the purpose but the receipts of live stock increased to such an extent that the facilities were soon found inadequate. . . .

The rapid development of the railroad lines entering the city had caused such a slowing down of freight and live stock in transit that the congestion was becoming a serious question. The idea of building a belt railroad was conceived by Joel F. Richardson, a practical railroad man, who had been the engineer on much of the construction work in Indiana. . . . He showed a map of what he called a "circle" railroad for Indianapolis, and unquestionably out of this plan grew the present Belt Railroad.[5]

So Indianapolis may be credited with conceiving the belt railroad idea; all indications are that a line around the city to avoid the downtown spaghetti bowl of tracks was first tried here. It was the 1870s before this happened, but the idea had been born more than twenty years earlier as a proposed belt line much closer to the city's center. In 1849, when the Madison & Indianapolis was still the city's only railroad, a plan called for a "common track encircling Indianapolis on North, South, East, and West Streets. . . . The Depots could be located on or near these streets, and the cars from any road could traverse them at pleasure, thereby virtually making the depot for each road a common depot, as the business man would deliver and receive his goods at the depot nearest his house."[6] (By "depot" the writer meant a freight depot, and by "house" a place of business, not a residence.) This plan went nowhere, apparently for good reason. First, the boundary streets of the Mile Square would have had tracks in them, creating an "ironbound" city center subject to the whims and delays of train movements. Then there was the fact that railroads seldom shared freight facilities such as the proposed "common depots." Competitive considerations, differences in freight and paperwork handling, and possible disputes over space needs and division of revenues all argued against sharing. In addition, the nightmare scenario of having to move cars from depot to depot so businessmen could ship and receive close to their businesses was too much to even consider.

This "circle line" proposal died aborning but surfaced again in the 1870s, when railroad congestion had become a serious issue. Around 1872 or 1873, a group of Indianapolis investors proposed a belt railroad to relieve the "very great and serious delays, risks and losses attend[ing] the transfer of freights in and through the city of Indianapolis, upon the tracks and lines of the several Railroads in consequence of the increasing number of the lines, and the rapid growth of their business, which has greatly outgrown their present means and facilities for transfer through the city."[7] The 1873 panic quashed this effort, but it arose again once the economy began to improve. Historian Berry Sulgrove told the story:

> A Belt Road, to connect outside of the city all the roads entering it, by which they could transfer cars and trains from one to the other without passing through the city, was projected and partly graded by a company, mainly composed of other railroad companies, eight or ten years ago, but abandoned in the stress of finances. In 1876 it was taken up by a company, mainly of capitalists in the city or connected with the railroads centering here, and on popular approval by a vote the city indorsed [sic] the company's bonds to the amount of five hundred thousand dollars, taking a mortgage on the road and stock to secure itself, and the road was rapidly built in connection with the stock-yard, and opened for business in November, 1877.[8]

No doubt the landing of enough public funding to cover almost the entire cost of the railroad helped to move things along. The new company, formed on August 29, 1876, proposed not only a belt line but also the stockyards to be served by the railroad. In the three years since the original effort failed, businessmen of Indianapolis had awakened to the opportunities in livestock and knew that efficient transportation was essential. The Union Railroad, Transfer, and Stock-Yard Company was organized under handwritten Articles of Association, in which nine directors were named: James C. Ferguson, John Thomas, William C. Holmes, E. F. Claypool, W. N. Jackson, John F. Miller, M. A. Downing, Horace (?) Scott, and W. R. McKeen. The articles then described the proposed railroad: "Said Railroad shall commence at a Point on the Indianapolis, Cincinnati, and La Fayette Railroad in North Indianapolis, Marion County, Indiana, thence in a southern, eastern, and northern direction to the Cleveland, Columbus, Cincinnati and Indianapolis Railroad in or near the town of Brightwood, around, near to and through the outskirts of the city of Indianapolis, passing through the County of Marion only, and the length of said road is about twelve miles."[9] As Sulgrove noted, the city's financial assistance enabled an immediate start to construction—a lucky break for sure since the disruptions of the 1873 panic had not yet settled out. Perhaps because of a residual bad taste from the days of the internal improvements mess, this was a controversial move that required skillful political maneuvering on the part of Mayor John Caven.

Work began immediately but soon came to a halt due to land acquisition problems that ended up in court. In early June of 1877, idle workers became restive over lost wages and inability to feed their families. This nearly coincided with the violent and destructive national railroad strike that July, which itself was in large part a result of economic decline due to the 1873 panic. The strike got wildly out of hand, particularly in Pittsburgh, where the extent of death and destruction was shocking. In Indianapolis, by contrast, Mayor Caven defused the danger by purchasing bread for workers with his own money and befriending local railroaders by enlisting them as guardians of railroad property; he also established a formal committee to hear grievances.[10] Work resumed and proceeded quickly as the crisis passed, and the railroad and the stockyards both opened for business on November 12, 1877. Even with delays, this first part of the belt railroad was built in about fifteen months.

An 1876 map of the city[11] shows the partially completed line. Its northern end was its connection with the Indianapolis, Bloomington & Western (IB&W; later the Peoria & Eastern), slightly north of West Washington Street. Shown as the "Indianapolis Belt Railroad," the line diverged from the IB&W and ran south-southeast, crossing at grade the Indianapolis & St. Louis (later the Big Four/New York Central) and the Terre Haute & Richmond (later the Pan Handle/Pennsylvania Railroad), with interchange tracks to both. Continuing to the south-southeast, the Belt crossed Judge Harding Street (now just Harding Street) and just below Morris Street turned eastward and crossed the Indianapolis & Vincennes (later the Pennsylvania) Railroad. From there to the White River was open land, part of which today is the site of the Lilly Industrial Center. It was here that the stockyards were built south of the Belt. Continuing southeast, the Belt track turned to the east just west of the White River, crossed the river, and ended at a junction with the Madison & Indianapolis Railroad about three blocks east of Meridian Street. This early segment was about a quarter of the Belt's eventual twelve-mile length and was intended to get the stockyards up and running while the rest of the line was built over the next few years.

An 1889 map shows the Belt twelve years on.[12] When completed it was single track over its full length from North Indianapolis along a U-shaped path to its termination at Brightwood on the northeast side of the city; it crossed all connecting railroads at grade, and a large loop of track served the stockyards. The map does not show the Belt's branch that connected with the Lake Erie & Western (LE&W) and the Monon, even though it opened in either 1884 or 1886, and there were other errors, too: the Belt is marked with an incorrect name, and the line that became the Monon is not shown, even though it was completed in 1883. The lesson here is that not all primary historical sources can be relied upon uncritically.

The Belt's first two annual reports provide a look at the road's early operations. The first, handwritten and two pages long, covered the period from the November 12, 1877, start of operations to December 31, 1878. Construction had cost $593,378.56; the stockyards were under construction at the same time and had cost $260,778.30. Floating debt totaled $88,818.82, against which the company held cash, receivables, and other cash assets of $47,438.77. During the thirteen months and eighteen days covered by the report, the railroad's revenues totaled $202,316.25. Operating expenses were $99,344.54, to which the company added $11,000.00 of general expenses, leaving net income of $91,971.71. Operation of the stockyards was similarly profitable. The report ended with justifiable optimism: "In view of the foregoing results, we may fairly claim that the business of the Company has been fully and successfully inaugurated, and that with the growth of this point as a [live]stock market may justly hope for a steady growth of the business of the Company."[13]

Figure 4.1 This map likely dates from the late 1870s, before the Union Railroad, Transfer & Stock-Yard Company changed its name to the Belt Railroad and Stock Yard Company. The company used the map in its annual reports for many years, but the early railroad names were never changed; see chapter 2 for help in unraveling the sometimes confusing string of corporate identities. The "LE&W Extension" of the Belt had not been built at the time the map was drawn.

Indiana Historical Society, HE2791

The above Map will be of interest to the public, in its correctness in noting the number of Railroads and the direction from which they enter the City, making Indianapolis a great Railroad Center, showing, also, the line of the Union Transfer Railroad, with its connections, the location of the Stock Yards connected therewith, &c.

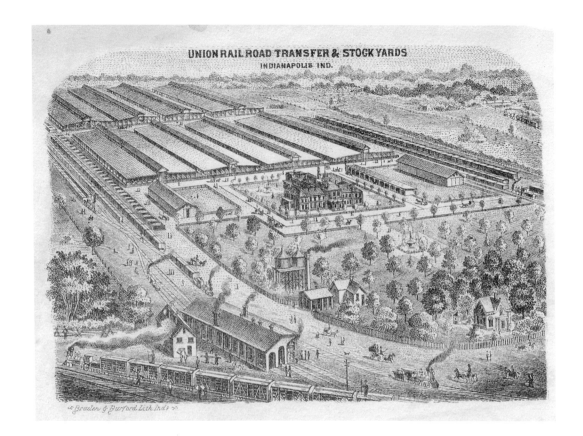

UNION RAIL ROAD TRANSFER & STOCK YARDS
INDIANAPOLIS IND.

Figure 4.2 Dating from about the same time as the Belt's map in figure 4.1, a bird's-eye view of the stockyards shows the Belt main line, early engine facilities, and the tracks serving the stockyards.

Indiana Historical Society

The report was signed by William Riley McKeen of Terre Haute, company president. He was the new belt line's principal organizer, a successful banker, and a formidable railroad manager.[14] The report for 1879 was even more glowing. More than 250,000 railroad cars were handled, an average of nearly 700 a day, and the stockyards received 1,370,417 head, nearly 3,800 a day; the care of the livestock required 1.5 million pounds of hay, 50,000 bushels of corn, and 3,000 bushels of oats. The report then closed with an item of interest: "We have been in perfect harmony with all Rail Road connections. . . . Manufactories of various kinds are springing up along our line and the prospects for largely increasing our business were never so promising as at the present time."[15] Like gas stations and motels attracted to an outer-belt freeway, within two years of the opening of the Belt

Figure 4.2A The engine terminal was always just east of Kentucky Avenue near the bottom of the "U" formed by the Belt's main line. Note that the 1870s engine house/machine shop was still active when this undated photo was made, and it would continue in use into the Conrail era. The view is to the east; north of the engine house is the wood coaling tower, and, just this side of it, the ash pit, ash conveyor, and loaded ash cars. IU locomotive number 5 simmers nearby in the afternoon sun.

Indiana Historical Society, M899

businesses were locating along it in a crescent-shaped industrial corridor outside downtown Indianapolis that still exists today.

In April of 1881 the Union Railroad, Transfer & Stock-Yard Company changed its name to the Belt Railroad and Stock Yard Company, perhaps to describe better its intended purpose, but likely also to avoid confusion with the Indianapolis Union Railway (IU). At that time the two operations were entirely separate. More change came on October 17, 1882, when the company leased the Belt to the IU Railway. The lease term was 999 years, with the stockyards expressly excluded. The Belt's founders must have felt more comfortable running only the stockyards and leaving the Belt to the IU's more experienced railroaders.

Figure 4.3 The Belt passed through rural countryside well into the twentieth century, before suburbanization forever altered such scenes. The photo may date from around the 1920s. Note the early version of automatic crossing protection. The caption says the location is 21st Street and Sherman Drive, which would place it at the Belt's east end near Eastside Junction. Direction of view is uncertain but appears to be to the south along Sherman at the crossing of the Lake Erie & Western Extension.

Indiana Historical Society, P0411

Extending the Belt

Because of where it was built, the Belt could not connect with two railroads that entered Indianapolis from the north: the Indianapolis, Peru & Chicago (IP&C; the former Peru & Indianapolis and later the Lake Erie & Western/Nickel Plate Road) and the Louisville, New Albany & Chicago (LNA&C; later the Monon). These lines were two miles west of the east leg of the Belt. To make a connection with them the Belt Railroad Company of Indianapolis was organized in 1883 by individuals involved with the Belt Railroad and Stock Yard Company. The new railroad was a branch of the Belt and was to extend about four miles west from near Brightwood to a connection with the Belt's west end at North Indianapolis. This would provide junctions with the IP&C and the LNA&C and also would close the rail circle around Indianapolis and give the Belt maximum flexibility in traffic dispatching. The first portion, connecting the Belt main line to the IP&C and the LNA&C, was completed in either 1884 or 1886, but track laying never went farther west. A good guess at the reason would note that the north side of the city by this time was beginning to grow with new residential construction, and land values were rising; this is where some of the most attractive neighborhoods of Indianapolis developed. Certainly in the 1880s plans would have been under way for such developments, likely by influential people who were not interested in having a railroad running nearby and who were in a position to see that it did not.

Even in its final if incomplete form the Belt served as a model for how a belt railroad could benefit a city and its line-haul railroads. It was built close to the city center but far enough out to avoid downtown rail traffic congestion; it was built on inexpensive rural land that required fewer negotiations and conflicts with landowners than on land closer in; it connected with all the city's railroads; and it was located so that those railroads could build freight yards near the Belt, cutting interchange time. The wisdom of the idea was proven by those first two annual reports showing remarkable traffic levels and financial results. The eventual construction of the more than two hundred other belt, terminal, switching, and connecting railroad companies cited in the 1947 Association of American Railroads publication[16] can be credited, at least in part if not entirely, to the Indianapolis Belt's having shown the way.

C-25779

With the IP&C/LE&W branch completed, the Belt's corporate evolution continued when the two companies consolidated as the "Belt Railroad and Stock Yard Company (No. 2)."[17] This entity in turn leased the new branch to the Indianapolis Union Railway Company for 999 years. So by the late 1880s the IU had operational control of the original Union Tracks, the 1888 Union Station, and both the original Belt Railroad and its "LE&W Extension"; it would retain this legal structure into the Conrail era.

The Belt Railroad in the ICC Valuation Records

The Interstate Commerce Commission (ICC) valuation records that helped tell the story of Union Station also had a detailed analysis of the Indianapolis Belt Railroad as it existed at the end of 1922. Because the Belt and its connecting railroads have changed so much since then, these documents help us understand the physical characteristics of the railroad at its maximum size and extent. Page A of the summary, typed on official ICC Division of Valuation graph paper, provides an interesting summary:[18]

C.C.C. & St. L. Ry. Jct., W. 26th Street to Brightwood Junction
1st Main(Sta. 0+00 to Sta. 635+01
(M.P. 0.000 to M.P. 12.027
2nd Main(Sta. 137+30 to Sta. 634+38
(M.P. 2.60 to M.P. 12.015

There is a lot of information in this brief tabulation. It tells us that the summary covered the Belt Railroad from its far west end at its junction with the old Chicago main line of the Big Four (New York Central) southward, eastward, and northward to its eastern termination at Brightwood, where it connected with the Big Four line to Bellefontaine and Cleveland. The entire length of the first or primary main line track was 63,501 feet, or 12.027 miles. The second main track did not begin until Station 137+30, or 13,730 feet from the beginning of the first main, 2.6 miles from the junction with the Big Four Chicago line. That second main track ended at Station 634+38, 63 feet short of the Big Four junction at Brightwood, where a switch on the Belt's second main track connected back into the first main just before that track joined the Big Four.

Page A of the summary also included the following:

L.E. & W. Extension
P. & E. East Side Jct. to L.E. & W. Junction
1st Main(Sta. 0+00 to Sta. 113+64
(M.P. 0.00 to M.P. 2.152
2nd Main(Sta. 0+29 to Sta. 113+64
(M.P. 0.005 to M.P. 2.152

In this case, the double-track extension diverged to the west from the Belt at East Side Junction, south of the Big Four's main line to Bellefontaine and Cleveland. This track curved north and west and immediately crossed the Big Four's line to Springfield, Ohio (the former Indianapolis, Bloomington & Western/Ohio, Indiana &Western/Peoria & Eastern, completed in 1882). The Belt extension paralleled this latter line until crossing the Big Four mains at DX Tower. It then continued straight west toward its junction with the Lake Erie & Western (the former Peru & Indianapolis, later the Nickel Plate and then the Norfolk &

Figure 4.4 A page from the Interstate Commerce Commission's inventory of the Belt (at that time formally called the Belt Railroad and Stock Yard Company) shows the great level of effort that went into this work, and why it is such a rich source of historical information. The location is the junction called Pine; the Belt runs north and south at the left, crossing over the Pennsylvania and the Baltimore & Ohio (at this time the Pittsburgh, Cincinnati, Chicago & St Louis and the Cincinnati, Indianapolis & Western/Cincinnati, Hamilton & Dayton, respectively), with connecting tracks to both. Note that north is at the bottom of the page.

ICC valuation map, Richard K. Baldwin collection

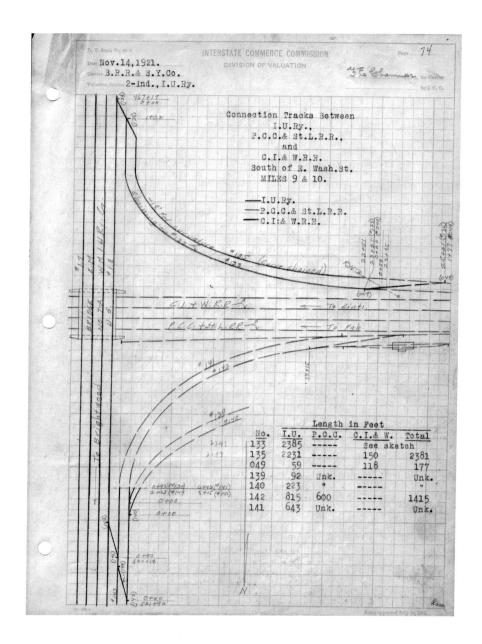

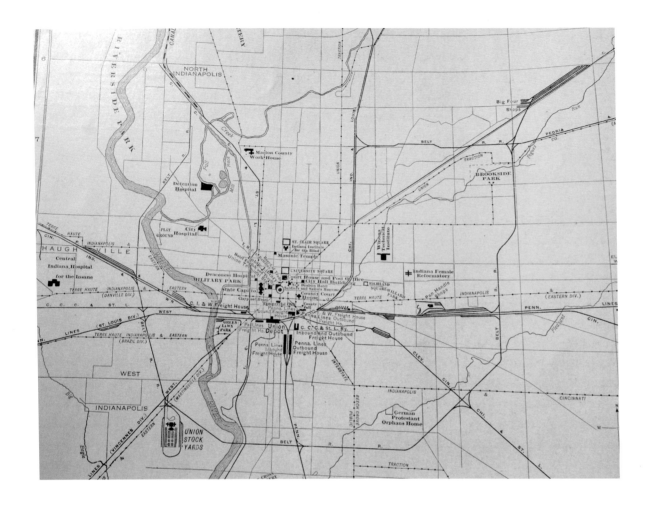

Figure 4.5 *Rand McNally & Company's Commercial Atlas of America* for 1918 contains this map of Indianapolis. Depiction of the Belt and its connecting railroads is largely correct, and it also shows the city's interurban lines. This was pretty much the peak for both types of rail transportation in terms of trackage and traffic.

Courtesy of RM Acquisition, LLC d/b/a Rand McNally, author's collection

Western); there also was a connecting track to the single-track Monon main line running parallel to and west of the LE&W.

Over the following ninety-six ICC graph-paper pages, the entire Belt Railroad was laid out in detail, drawn and lettered in pencil and colored ink, showing all the junctions with other railroads and with mileposts and station numbers carefully noted; it showed major features, including grade crossings, bridges, culverts, buildings, and signals; and it had accurate and detailed schematic layouts of the various junctions, sidings, and industry spur leads. It did not identify on-line customers, but the welter of main tracks, spur tracks, passing tracks, and switching leads depicted in this document clearly suggests how busy this small railroad once was.

By 1922 the Belt had largely become the double-track railroad promised by its founders. Double-tracking occurred early on: the 1889 city map shows double track extending from milepost 2.6 all the way around to what would become Pan Handle Junction, the crossing of the Pennsylvania Railroad's Pittsburgh line on the east side of the city. The single track north from that point was later made double for nearly its entire length. The Belt identified its tracks by numbered segments called "switches," which are not to be confused with track switches (also called turnouts). The term appears to have been applied not only to industrial spurs but also to segments of main lines, sidings, and yard tracks. Each was numbered, beginning at the west end of the line. Two spur tracks, or switches, at Station 76+07, for example, were designated #11 and #12. Eventually several hundred "switch" numbers covered all of the Belt's trackage. Presumably these designations helped make clear what specific piece of track was being referred to in train orders, switching lists, car-mile accounting, and other references to specific locations on the Belt.

The Belt connected with all the railroads it crossed. Its west end connection was with the Big Four's Chicago line, which was later replaced by a new line farther west but survived into the 1990s as a spur track into the downtown area. Then, moving "railroad east," it crossed the Peoria & Eastern and the B&O at KD; the Big Four's St. Louis line at BX (which stood for "Belt Crossing"), later CP 1 (Control Point 1); then only about 600 feet to the south was Woods, also called Vandalia Crossing, derived from both the corporate and the popular name for the Pan Handle/Pennsylvania Railroad's St. Louis line. The multiple tracks on all three railroads at these last two crossings, along with several multiple interchange tracks, suggest the density of the traffic here. Both the Big Four and the PRR lines were major routes and would have been the most active interchanges on the western half of the Belt. To accommodate this traffic density the four-track Belt had eastward (toward Brightwood) and westward (toward North Indianapolis) main lines on the inner tracks, and sidings called "runners" on the outer tracks to permit interchange and industry switching without fouling the mains.

The teams preparing the Interstate Commerce Commission (ICC)'s 1920s valuation of railroad properties were not known for a high level of photographic skill, but they did create a tremendous resource for later historians. There is probably no better collection of images of the Belt's trackside structures than the one assembled for the ICC. Following are several images depicting some of the modest facilities of the Belt. Interlocking towers at crossings with other railroads were owned by those roads and not by the Belt, but they certainly could be considered a part of the Belt's physical fabric.

Figure 4.6 At West Michigan Street a well-hatted and bundled-up crossing guard posed proudly with the stop sign she used to keep motorists and pedestrians off the Belt's track. This location is just south of today's Cargill grain plant on the city's west side.

ICC valuation photo,
Richard K. Baldwin collection

Figure 4.7 Not far south of West Michigan Street was Moorefield Junction, the Belt's connection with the Baltimore & Ohio Railroad. Note the outdoor arrangement of levers controlling the switches and signals here; winter must have made life interesting for the operator.

ICC valuation photo,
Richard K. Baldwin collection

Figure 4.8 At Vandalia Junction, also known as Woods, the Belt crossed and connected with the Pan Handle route of the Pennsylvania Railroad. The PRR provided its operators a more substantial tower than the one back at Moorefield Junction.

ICC valuation photo, Richard K. Baldwin collection

Figure 4.9 Just west of the Belt at Woods, this little structure was identified as a "signal repairman's house." It actually is along the Pennsylvania tracks but might have been used by both the Belt and the PRR. Note the nice touch of the gable ornamentation.

ICC valuation photo,
Richard K. Baldwin collection

Figure 4.10 Where it crossed the Belt, Morris Street was guarded by an elevated crossing tower. Access to such buildings typically was by a ladder up through the floor. Crossing gates would have been controlled from the tower so the guard did not have to negotiate the ladder for every train.

ICC valuation photo, Richard K. Baldwin collection

Figure 4.11 This slightly blurred view looks southwest at the yard office ("yardmaster's and trainmaster's office," according to the ICC photographer) just east of Kentucky Avenue. Yard tracks and the Belt's engine terminal were to the east of this point, and the stockyards were to the south. The ornate entrance gate to the stockyards is in the left background behind the office.

ICC valuation photo, Richard K. Baldwin collection

Figure 4.12 Looking better built than the frame buildings the IU seemed to favor, the oil house at the line's engine terminal was of brick construction, probably for fire prevention. Even more interesting are the tin lizzies parked around it.

ICC valuation photo, Richard K. Baldwin collection

Figure 4.13 As long as there was an engine terminal along the Belt, this was its machine shop and engine house, an enlarged version of the same building shown in figure 4.2. This view is to the northwest.

ICC valuation photo, Richard K. Baldwin collection

Figure 4.14 Twin water towers slaked the thirst of the IU's switcher fleet in steam days. Some of the stockyard sheds are in the background.

ICC valuation photo, Richard K. Baldwin collection

Figure 4.15 The wooden coaling tower (or "coal wharf" to the CC photographer) was replaced in later years by a modern steel one. It can be seen in the background of figure 4.29.

ICC valuation photo, Richard K. Baldwin collection

Figure 4.16 A dual ash hoist helped the IU dispose of the prodigious amounts of ash produced by its steam fleet.

ICC valuation photo, Richard K. Baldwin collection

Figure 4.17 IU buildings included this classic privy—no doubt a "one-holer"—at Singleton Street. Nothing was too small to escape the eagle eye of the Interstate Commerce Commission.

ICC valuation photo, Richard K. Baldwin collection

The Belt then crossed the I&V, the PRR's single-track line to Vincennes, at Vincennes Junction near Kentucky Avenue. The I&V later became an industrial spur known as both the Old Vincennes Main and the Caven Industrial Spur. There were eight Belt tracks at this point because both the stockyard leads and the Belt's engine terminal and shop were located east of Kentucky Avenue. The engine and shop facilities were north and a little east of the stockyards and included a yardmaster's office, coal house, toilet, trainmen's office, water tanks, coal dock, sand and oil houses, shop, and boiler room. Many of these would last well into the post–World War II era. East of the engine terminal and shop, in keeping with the nearby land use, was a crossover (a connection between parallel tracks) called Abbatoir.

To the east, the larger of the Belt's two White River bridges was at about milepost 5.1. In 1922 this was a three-span double-track steel through truss bridge with a wood pile trestle eastern approach; total length was close to 600 feet. In 1930 the American Bridge Company replaced this structure with a four-track eight-span deck plate girder bridge, which remains in use today. Just east of the bridge was the interchange with the Illinois Central line from Effingham, Illinois. Because of the elevation of the bridge over the White River, the Belt was on a high embankment that took it over the IC.

Past Meridian Street the Belt next crossed the PRR's Louisville line (the original Madison & Indianapolis) at grade, a point called Dale, then a little farther on crossed East Street at milepost 6. Just after milepost 7 and the State Street grade crossing, the line curved northeast to Belt Crossing, the connection with the Big Four's Hill Yard and the Big Four line to Cincinnati. To the

southeast some distance beyond the yard were the Big Four car shops at Beech Grove, opened in 1908 and still used by Amtrak. Back on the Belt, next came the connection with the Pennsylvania Railroad and its Hawthorne Yard. Opened in 1917, this two-mile-long freight yard, intended to reduce congestion and speed up the sorting and forwarding of freight cars on the PRR's Pan Handle line between Pittsburgh and St. Louis, was about three-fourths of a mile to the south of the PRR main line. The Belt reached the west end of the yard by means of a wye, the south leg of which was called Prospect Wye and the north Hamilton Wye. On the Belt just north of the Hamilton Wye was Hamilton Junction, where the Belt connected with both the B&O's line to Hamilton and Cincinnati and the Pan Handle main line. At a location on those two railroads known as Pine, a connecting track descended from the Belt embankment and then turned west to connect with and cross the B&O at grade; it then connected with the Pan Handle. An eastbound train on the Pan Handle entered Hawthorne Yard by diverging southward at Pine, crossing the B&O, curving south while moving uphill on the Belt connection, and then negotiating the crossovers that took it around Hamilton Wye to reach the west leads of the yard. This was the most complicated railroad connection on the Belt. Hawthorne Yard's east end was about six miles east of Union Station; the yard's east lead tracks connected to the Pan Handle main line at a junction called Thorne.

The Belt crossed above both the PRR and the B&O at Pine. Milepost 10 was about a half mile north of Pine, and at milepost 11.25 the first of the diverging tracks at Eastside Junction left the main. This connection was where the double track of the LE&W Extension left the Belt and curved to the west, first crossing the single track of the Peoria & Eastern line to Ohio and then the double track of the Big Four's Cleveland line at DX Tower. Then, less than a mile farther on, the Belt's main line ended without much fanfare at Belt Junction. The two main tracks curved eastward and then converged to one track right at milepost 12, just before crossing Massachusetts Avenue and connecting with the Big Four's eastbound main. And so terminated the Indianapolis Belt Railroad of the early 1920s, built up from the spindly little single-track hog-hauler of 1877 into a robust freight handler ready for the ever-growing traffic that, at the time, seemed assured for years to come.

BUSINESS ON THE BELT

Over the years, industries of all kinds and sizes located along the Belt. A complete list, which could be assembled with enough time and effort, would be quite long and would easily illustrate why the Belt's single main track soon became double, and why so many passing sidings were built to facilitate local switching. With frequent through trains, transfer runs between the various railroads, and local industry switching, the Belt seemed always to have something in motion on its tracks. It all started with the stockyards but, as intended by the founders, grew rapidly from that one customer. Files of the Indianapolis Union Railway have been preserved in both public and private collections and are replete with correspondence, budgets, authorizations for expenditure, and engineering drawings covering track leases, industrial spur construction, and land acquisitions, disposals, and leases—myriad transactions and improvements undertaken to accommodate the needs of the Belt's shifting list of customers over the years.

Those customers were a blend of local enterprises, regional operations, and national firms: Metal Auto Parts Company, Citizens Gas and Coke, Dependable Coal Company, National Lead Company, Seery Lumber Company, the Glidden Company Feed Mill Division, Liquid Sugars, Inc., RCA Victor Division of Radio Corporation of America. Customers and railroad connections were published periodically on the IU Railway Company's Form 400, "Station Numbers—Belt Railroad." Some firms shown on these sheets from sixty-plus years ago are with us today (Carter Lee Lumber Company, for example), or remain in operation under a new name (National Starch Products, Inc., now Ingredion, Inc.).

In 1956 the Railroad Community Committee of Indianapolis published a small guidebook for passengers taking a special excursion on the Belt. Titled *The Belt Railroad—Industrial Lifeline of Indianapolis*, it briefly recounted the histories of the Union Railway, Union Station, and the Belt and noted that as of 1956 there were 152 industries served by the Belt on 115 private sidings.[19] This was accomplished by 27 weekday crews and 11 Sunday crews operating 12 diesel-electric locomotives. Lifeline, indeed. This was one busy railroad. 1956, though, probably was the high-water mark in the Belt's customer count and traffic levels. The interstate highway system got under way that year; its effects would come slowly but no less surely, including among its impacts the outward movement of industry to truck-served "greenfield" sites beyond the central area of Indianapolis and far away from the sidings and spur tracks of the Belt. Still, as late as mid-1966, the line's station numbers list included around a hundred rail customers.

Map 4.1 through Map 4.4 These four maps show the growth and decline of the Belt Railroad over nearly 140 years. The fledgling line of 1877 served mainly the new stockyards, indicated by the two spur lines west of the White River on the southwest side of the city. By 1918 the railroad had reached full flower, and it remained fairly intact until after the late 1970s. From then until today, as with railroads all over the country, there was a great deal of "rationalization" as former trunk lines were abandoned and trackside industries closed or moved away. Contraction of the Belt was unavoidable; however, even though its west end today is out of service, its original main line remains in place.

Map 4.1

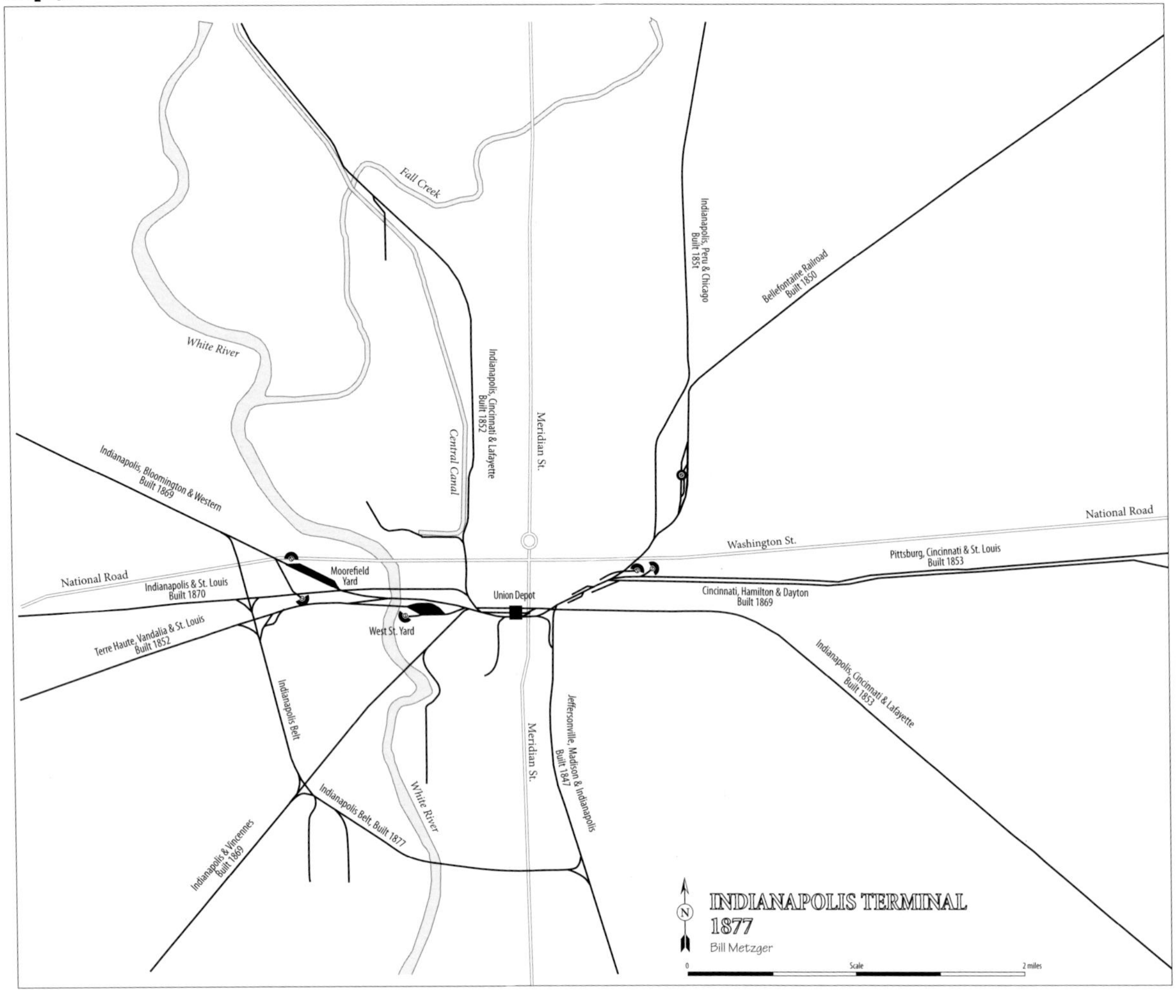

Fall Creek

White River

Indianapolis, Peru & Chicago Built 1851

Bellefontaine Railroad Built 1850

Indianapolis, Cincinnati & Lafayette Built 1852

Central Canal

Meridian St.

National Road

Washington St.

Pittsburg, Cincinnati & St. Louis Built 1853

Indianapolis, Bloomington & Western Built 1869

National Road

Indianapolis & St. Louis Built 1870

Moorefield Yard

Union Depot

Cincinnati, Hamilton & Dayton Built 1869

Terre Haute, Vandalia & St. Louis Built 1852

West St. Yard

Indianapolis, Cincinnati & Lafayette Built 1853

Indianapolis Belt

Indianapolis & Vincennes Built 1869

Indianapolis Belt Built 1877

White River

Meridian St.

Jeffersonville, Madison & Indianapolis Built 1847

INDIANAPOLIS TERMINAL
1877
Bill Metzger

N

0   Scale   2 miles

Map 4.2

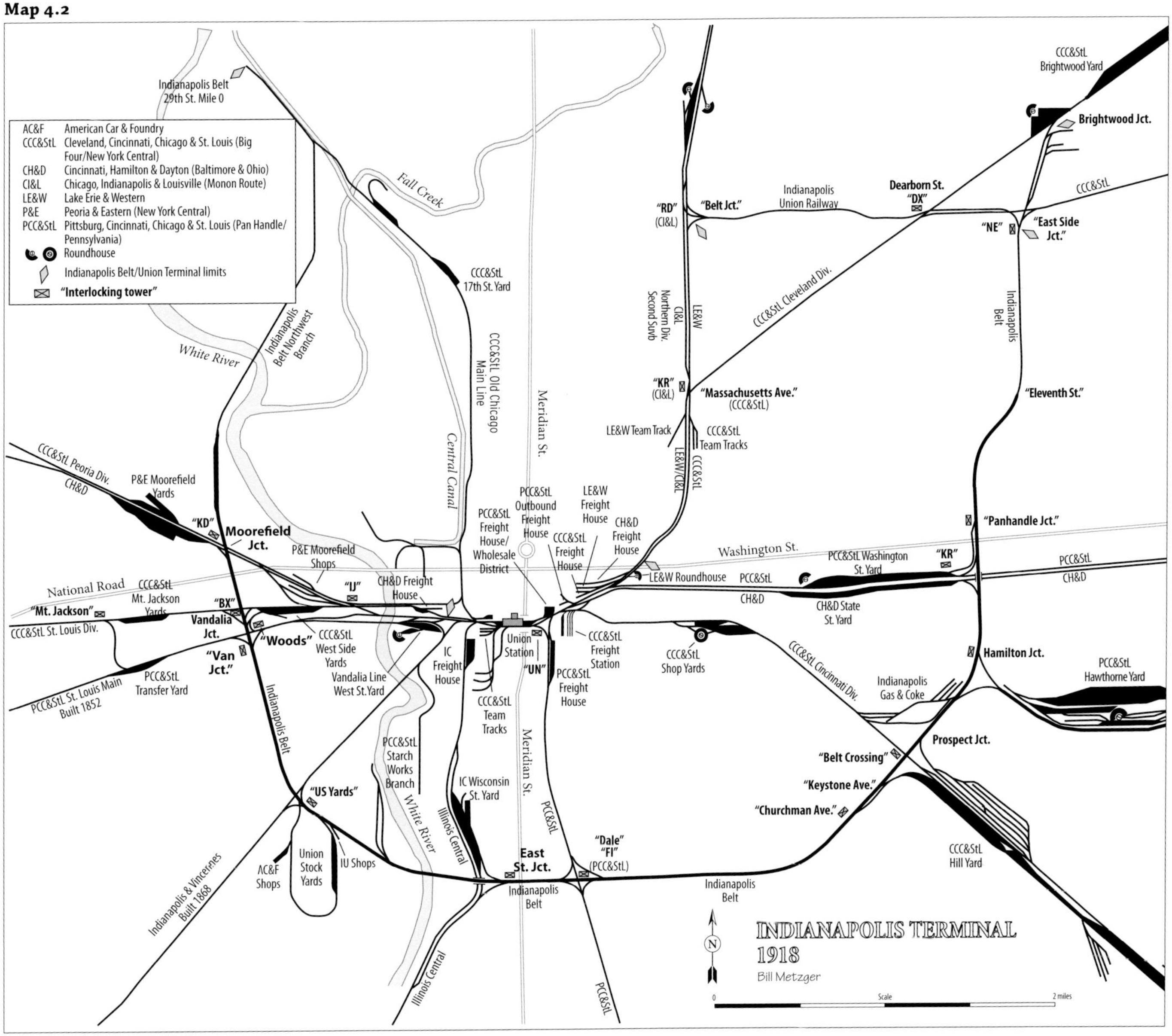
AC&F American Car & Foundry
CCC&StL Cleveland, Cincinnati, Chicago & St. Louis (Big Four/New York Central)
CH&D Cincinnati, Hamilton & Dayton (Baltimore & Ohio)
CI&L Chicago, Indianapolis & Louisville (Monon Route)
LE&W Lake Erie & Western
P&E Peoria & Eastern (New York Central)
PCC&StL Pittsburg, Cincinnati, Chicago & St. Louis (Pan Handle/ Pennsylvania)
Roundhouse
Indianapolis Belt/Union Terminal limits
"Interlocking tower"
INDIANAPOLIS TERMINAL 1918
Bill Metzger
Scale
0
2 miles
N
Indianapolis Belt 29th St. Mile 0
Fall Creek
CCC&StL 17th St. Yard
CCC&StL Old Chicago Main Line
Meridian St.
Central Canal
White River
Indianapolis Belt Northwest Branch
CCC&StL Peoria Div.
CH&D
P&E Moorefield Yards
"KD"
Moorefield Jct.
P&E Moorefield Shops
National Road
CCC&StL Mt. Jackson Yards
"Mt. Jackson"
CCC&StL St. Louis Div.
"BX"
Vandalia Jct.
"Woods"
"Van Jct."
PCC&StL Transfer Yard
PCC&StL St. Louis Main Built 1852
CCC&StL West Side Yards
Vandalia Line West St. Yard
"U"
CH&D Freight House
Indianapolis Belt
"US Yards"
AC&F Shops
Union Stock Yards
IU Shops
Indianapolis & Vincennes Built 1868
PCC&StL Starch Works Branch
IC Freight House
Illinois Central
IC Wisconsin St. Yard
CCC&StL Team Tracks
Union Station
"UN"
PCC&StL Freight House
CCC&StL Freight Station
PCC&StL Freight House/ Wholesale District
PCC&StL Outbound Freight House
LE&W Freight House
CCC&StL Freight House
CH&D Freight House
Washington St.
LE&W Roundhouse
PCC&StL
CH&D
PCC&StL Washington St. Yard
CH&D State St. Yard
"KR"
CCC&StL Shop Yards
CCC&StL Cincinnati Div.
Indianapolis Gas & Coke
East St. Jct.
Indianapolis Belt
"Dale" "FI" (PCC&StL)
PCC&StL
"Belt Crossing"
"Keystone Ave."
"Churchman Ave."
Prospect Jct.
CCC&StL Hill Yard
PCC&StL Hawthorne Yard
Hamilton Jct.
"Panhandle Jct."
"Eleventh St."
Indianapolis Belt
"NE"
"East Side Jct."
CCC&StL
Dearborn St. "DX"
Indianapolis Union Railway
"Belt Jct."
"RD" (CI&L)
CI&L Northern Div. Second Suvb
LE&W
CCC&StL Cleveland Div.
"KR" (CI&L)
"Massachusetts Ave." (CCC&StL)
LE&W Team Track
CCC&StL Team Tracks
LE&W/CI&L
CCC&StL
CCC&StL Brightwood Yard
Brightwood Jct.

Map 4.3

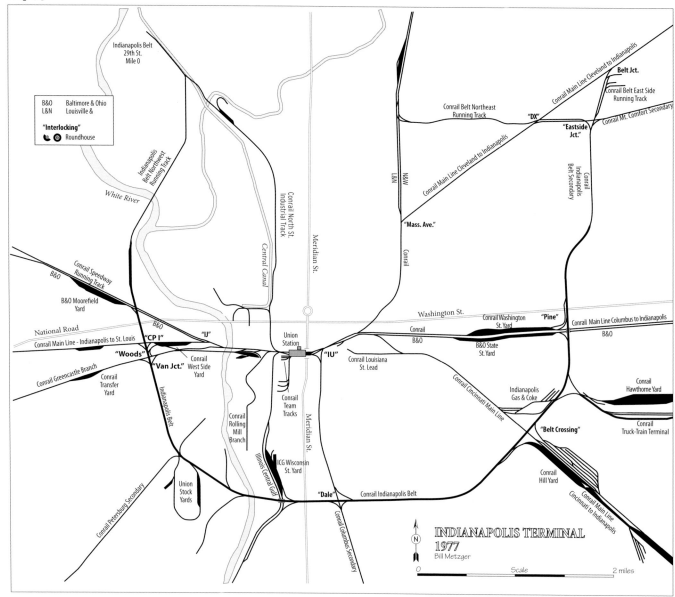

Indianapolis Belt
29th St.
Mile 0

B&O — Baltimore & Ohio
L&N — Louisville &

"Interlocking"
🚂 ◎ Roundhouse

Indianapolis Belt Northwest Running Track

White River

Conrail North St. Industrial Track

Meridian St.

Central Canal

Conrail Belt Northeast Running Track

Conrail Main Line Cleveland to Indianapolis

Conrail Main Line Cleveland to Indianapolis

Belt Jct.

Conrail Belt East Side Running Track

"DX"

"Eastside Jct."

Conrail Mt. Comfort Secondary

Conrail Indianapolis Belt Secondary

N&W
L&N

"Mass. Ave."

Conrail

Conrail Speedway Running Track
B&O

B&O Moorefield Yard

National Road

Conrail Main Line - Indianapolis to St. Louis

B&O

"CP I"

"IJ"

"Woods"

"Van Jct."

Conrail Greencastle Branch

Conrail West Side Yard

Conrail Transfer Yard

Union Station

Union Station

"IU"

Washington St.

Conrail Washington St. Yard

"Pine"

Conrail Main Line Columbus to Indianapolis

Conrail

B&O

B&O

B&O State St. Yard

Conrail Louisiana St. Lead

Conrail Cincinnati Main Line

Indianapolis Gas & Coke

Conrail Hawthorne Yard

Conrail Truck-Train Terminal

Indianapolis Belt

Conrail Rolling Mill Branch

Conrail Team Tracks

Meridian St.

Illinois Central Gulf

ICG Wisconsin St. Yard

"Belt Crossing"

Conrail Hill Yard

Conrail Petersburg Secondary

Union Stock Yards

"Dale"

Conrail Indianapolis Belt

Conrail Columbus Secondary

Conrail Main Line Cincinnati to Indianapolis

N

INDIANAPOLIS TERMINAL
1977
Bill Metzger

0   Scale   2 miles

Map 4.4

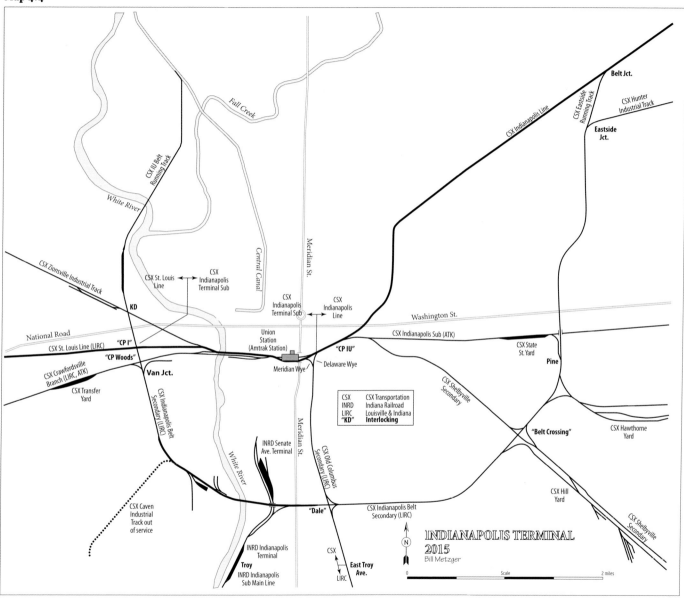

Fall Creek

CSX IU Belt Running Track

White River

CSX Indianapolis Line

Belt Jct.

CSX Eastside Running Track

CSX Hunter Industrial Track

Eastside Jct.

Central Canal

Meridian St.

CSX Zionsville Industrial Track

CSX St. Louis Line

CSX Indianapolis Terminal Sub

KD

CSX Indianapolis Terminal Sub

CSX Indianapolis Line

Washington St.

National Road

CSX St. Louis Line (LIRC)

"CP I"

Union Station (Amtrak Station)

CSX Indianapolis Sub (ATK)

CSX State St. Yard

"CP Woods"

CSX Crawfordsville Branch (LIRC, ATK)

Van Jct.

"CP IU"

Pine

Meridian Wye

Delaware Wye

CSX Transfer Yard

CSX Indianapolis Belt Secondary (LIRC)

CSX Shelbyville Secondary

CSX	CSX Transportation
INRD	Indiana Railroad
LIRC	Louisville & Indiana
"KD"	**Interlocking**

CSX Hawthorne Yard

INRD Senate Ave. Terminal

"Belt Crossing"

White River

Meridian St.

CSX Old Columbus Secondary (LIRC)

CSX Hill Yard

CSX Caven Industrial Track out of service

"Dale"

CSX Indianapolis Belt Secondary (LIRC)

CSX Shelbyville Secondary

INRD Indianapolis Terminal

Troy

INRD Indianapolis Sub Main Line

CSX

East Troy Ave.

LIRC

INDIANAPOLIS TERMINAL 2015
Bill Metzger

N

0   Scale   2 miles

Figure 4.18 (*Facing*) Looking east on Prospect Street on the city's southeast side, Dick Baldwin caught one of the New York Central's Mohawks with a Cincinnati-bound train. Belt Crossing tower is off to the right, and the gas and coke company plant forms the backdrop. It is November 3, 1954; time is short for the NYC's superpower.

Richard K. Baldwin photo

Figure 4.19 (*Above*) A little east of Belt Crossing, NYC Mohawk number 3123 brings a 1954 baseball special around the wye from the Belt onto the Big Four's Cincinnati line. Once again the massive gas and coke plant dominates the background.

Ron Stuckey photo, John Fuller collection

Figure 4.20 First with steam, then with diesel power, the Belt did its job week in and week out. A gloomy day late in 1957 finds New York Central's hotshot freight NY-6 passing the tower at Belt Junction as it crosses over the Big Four westbound main to enter Brightwood Yard. At Brightwood the Belt could pick up or deliver cars headed to industries on its line or to other railroad connections.

Jay Williams photo

Figure 4.21 IU number 14, the first unit in the railroad's second order of H-10-44s from Fairbanks-Morse, is trundling along with a long transfer run near Pine Junction. The "porch roof" that made these units so distinctive is readily apparent, as are the safety stripes added by the railroad after delivery. This model's carbody was the work of Raymond Loewy, well-known industrial designer.

Jay Williams collection

Figure 4.22 IU number 13 is dropping three hopper cars of coal at one of the small Indianapolis coal yards that once dotted the city. Location and date were not noted by the photographer, but it was likely in the late 1950s.

Ron Stuckey photo, John Fuller collection

The decline from that point, however, seems to have been precipitous. This was a national trend, of course—the migration of freight traffic, especially high-value products, from rail to truck transport occurred over the course of many years but was accelerated in the 1960s and 1970s by the interstate highway system. This new reality was most acute in the northeast quadrant of the country, where states such as Indiana, Ohio, Pennsylvania, New York, and New Jersey proved to have far too much railroad track for the traffic still available to them. A suffocating regulatory environment, high taxes, and heavy passenger train expenses made the situation even worse. In Indianapolis the effect of these forces could be read in the changing infrastructure of the Belt, a microcosm of what was happening across the country.

POWERING THE BELT

The Belt was entirely a steam railroad until 1948, when it placed its first diesel order. Its earliest locomotives likely were standard "American" type 4–4–0s, but by the late nineteenth or early twentieth century the railroad had turned to a fleet of 0–6–0

switch engines.[20] By 1927 the Belt had sixteen of them on its roster, along with six 0–8–0 switchers. These locomotives were purchased in small groups between 1902 and 1927 from four different builders. The 0–6–0 switchers numbered 3 through 5 came from American Locomotive Company's Schenectady works in 1902; numbers 7 through 9, also from Alco Schenectady, were built in 1903; 0–6–0s 18 and 20 were Schenectady products from 1905; and the final Schenectady 0–6–0, number 6, arrived in 1924. In 1907 Alco's Cooke works delivered numbers 21, 22, and 23, all 0–6–0s; and the final locomotives of this wheel arrangement, numbers 24 through 27, were built at the Pennsylvania Railroad's Juniata shops in Altoona, Pennsylvania, in 1911. Baldwin 0–8–0 number 1 was built in mid-1927 and was followed by 0–8–0s numbered 28 through 32 late that same year. The valuation record for these locomotives did not indicate which were bought new and which had earlier owners, although builders' photos confirm that numbers 1 and 28 were built for the IU, and numbers 29–32 very likely were as well. Gaps in the numbering suggest that some power had been retired, along with

Figure 4.23 Historical sources suggest that the Belt's earliest power was American-type 4–4–0s, a common locomotive type until after the Civil War. By the early twentieth century the Belt had turned to 0–6–0 switchers, some of them built in the previous century. One example was number 7, a Baldwin product from 1898. In this first 1925 photo, its time on the Belt was about up.

Jay Williams collection

Figure 4.24 IU number 32, the last purchased of its steam switchers, was built by the Lima Locomotive Works in 1927. Around 1948 it was simmering away while awaiting an assignment at the Monon's 27th Street yard.

Jay Williams collection

160

Figures 4.25 and 4.26 Although IU 0–8–0s numbers 1 and 28 were far apart in numbering, they arrived on the railroad within months of each other. Number 1, the road's only Baldwin steamer at the time, came in mid-1927. Number 28, a Lima product, and sisters numbers 29–32 came later that same year. All steam was gone from the Belt by the early 1950s.

Brian Banta collection

their numbers; and low-numbered power with late construction dates (numbers 1 and second 7, for example) probably filled slots vacated by retired units.

Additional 0–8–0 purchases came in 1930, by which time some of the oldest power was being retired. At the end of World War II, eleven steam engines, all lettered "Indianapolis Union Railway," served the company, and it had fourteen by early 1950. A few of the latter lasted into the diesel era but were retired in the early 1950s.[21]

The 1948 diesel order was given to Fairbanks-Morse and Company; during 1949 it delivered four of its model H-10-44 switch engines to the IU. Numbered 10 through 13, they were followed by five more, numbers 14 through 18, during 1950. Then in 1952 the railroad bought three of F-M's model H-12-44 switcher (which had 200 more horsepower than the first members of the fleet), numbered 19 through 21. By then the last of steam had been put out to pasture.

There were no further locomotive purchases until 1966, when the IU switched locomotive suppliers. Turning to the Electro-Motive Division of the General Motors Corporation, the railroad acquired two of EMD's SW1500 switch engines, numbered 22 and

23. Between 1967 and 1972, nine more of the same model followed, numbered 24 through 32. Once the EMD roster was filled out, IU was able to return some leased Penn Central units. All the F-M and EMD units were lettered for the IU.

The first nine of the F-M switchers were traded to EMD when the SW units were ordered; all were later scrapped, as were the final three of the F-Ms. All eleven of the EMD locomotives became Conrail units after the IU was folded into Conrail in 1977, following which the IU units were dispersed across the system and by the late 1990s had been sold to various railroads, short lines, and a locomotive leasing company.[22]

OPERATING THE BELT

The Indianapolis Belt Railroad was intended to carry three kinds of freight traffic: tenant railroads' trains bypassing downtown Indianapolis (the IU Railway for a long time discouraged freight traffic on the Union Tracks); cars being interchanged among the various railroads; and pickup and delivery of cars for customers along the Belt's tracks. The tenant railroads had equal access to customers on the Belt and paid an equal annual portion of a "fixed rental" of 7 percent of the value of the Belt's property.

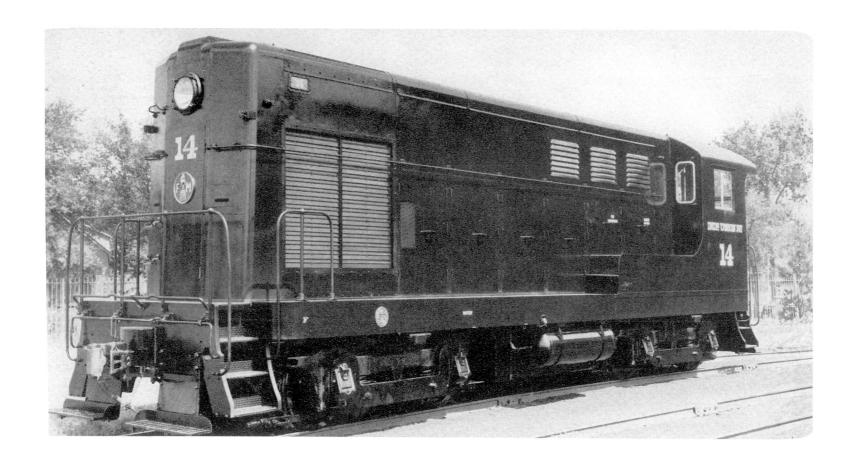

Figure 4.27 When dieselization came to the Belt in 1948, it was in the form of four Fairbanks-Morse H-10-44s, numbered 10–13. In 1950, five more, 14–18, followed, completing the railroad's roster of these models. The builder's photo of number 14 shows it as delivered without the safety stripes it would wear later on.

Brian Banta collection

Figure 4.28 IU number 21, photographed around 1960, was the Belt's last purchase from Fairbanks-Morse, arriving on the property in 1952 along with numbers 19 and 20. These three were F-M's H-12-44 model, 200 horsepower stronger than the H-10-44; most versions of this model lacked the rear "porch roof." There would be no more locomotive purchases until the first of the Electro-Motive Division SW-1500s arrived in 1966.

Ron Stuckey photo, John Fuller collection

Figure 4.29 On a sunny day around 1950 the IU posed four of its new and almost-new diesels by the soon-to-be-obsolete coaling tower at the road's engine terminal near the stockyards. Number 10 needed more side striping before it could match its sisters.

Jay Williams collection

Figure 4.30 Arriving in 1966, IU numbers 22 and 23 were the first EMD SW-1500s purchased by the Belt to begin the replacement of its first-generation F-M power.

Ron Stuckey photo, John Fuller collection

Figure 4.31 The Belt (actually its lessee, the Indianapolis Union Railway) had a remarkably varied caboose fleet. One was this little bobber number 102, undoubtedly from the nineteenth century but used into the 1950s. Here it looks like the work of a skilled model railroader. A more conventional center-cupola caboose (also known on various railroads as a hack, van, crummy, cabin car, etc.) sits in the background.

Ron Stuckey photo, John Fuller collection

Figure 4.32 IU caboose number 133, another wood car without a cupola, was more commodious than the bobber and also was a real survivor. A trackside rock-thrower has found his mark. Stenciling on the air reservoir is dated 1969.

Mont Switzer photo

Figure 4.33 The IU did have some more modern cabooses on the Belt, although even up-to-date steel bay window car number 250 still had a coal stove, as evidenced by the rooftop smoke jack.

Mont Switzer photo

Each railroad also paid a "wheelage," or car-mile, charge to cover operating expenses, figured periodically by dividing operating costs by the miles traveled by cars of each railroad.

The IU Railway Company's "Rules and Regulations" dated January 1, 1891, give a good picture of Belt operations at that time. Cars moving between railroads or going to or from Belt customers had to be handled only by Belt locomotives. Through traffic, that is, trains staying on a given railroad but using the Belt as a bypass around the city, "may pass over the Belt between junction points of such company, but shall not do any way or interchange work, except to leave Stock at Stock Yards." Penciled in after these last words was the notation "from inbound trains."[23] This policy would last until the Belt was absorbed by Penn Central in 1968. Prior to that time, it appears that the Pennsylvania and New York Central railroads, in particular, took seriously the Belt's reluctance to host freight traffic on the downtown Union Tracks. Various PRR and NYC system maps showed the U-shaped Belt as part of those roads' main lines through Indianapolis and downplayed the more direct route using IU's tracks.

The 1891 Rules and Regulations also stated that no trains would run on a schedule, "but the service shall be so arranged as may be required to furnish prompt and efficient deliveries." That is, all trains were to be run as unscheduled extras and, while the Belt published regulations and rule books from time to time, there never was an actual employee timetable. The Belt was dispatched entirely by a manual block system by which tower operators and switchmen at various points had authority over train movements. There were signals along the line, but they were neither automatic block nor centralized traffic control signals. They provided only distant and home protection for at-grade crossings with other railroads. Originally of the semaphore type, they were later replaced by a mix of both mast- and ground-mounted ("dwarf") color-light signals. The 1891 Rules and Regulations also addressed the receiving and delivery tracks to be provided by the various railroads; how cars were to be arranged for efficient transit and switching on the Belt; and how repairs to damaged cars would be handled.

Some twenty years later, operations were much the same, and would continue so for the life of the Belt. The IU Railway's rulebook of 1910 had twenty-four rules under the heading "Movement of Trains," among them #27: "No time-table is issued for the movement of trains on either double or single tracks. All trains are considered as extra, regardless of classification signals, and will be designated by the number and initial of the engine."[24]

Figures 4.34 and 4.35 (*Above and Facing*) In late September of 1951 the Cincinnati Railroad Club ran an excursion to Indianapolis for a visit to the Belt's engine terminal and the IC's Senate Avenue yard. The *James Whitcomb Riley* took the travelers to Union Station, where Indianapolis Railways buses were waiting to take them around the city. The IU forgot to park 0–8–0 number 6 in a "rods-down" position but thoughtfully opened the hood doors on F-M number 12 so its inner workings were visible.

C. A. Buehler photos, Gary Rolih collection

Figure 4.36 By the late 1950s or early 1960s the IU engine house/machine shop's doorways had been altered from their original arched form, though otherwise the building looked much as it had for nearly a century. The Belt main line runs behind the building, up on a low embankment.

Ron Stuckey photo, John Fuller collection

Figure 4.37 The IU's celebration of the nation's bicentennial included patriotic repainting of one of the SW-1500s but not maintenance of the original engine house and machine shop. Roof failure and trees growing out of the brickwork indicate that the building does not have a bright future.

Ron Stuckey photo, John Fuller collection

Figure 4.38 (*Facing*) It's 1969, the Belt is a Penn Central property, and the shanty at East Street shows some deferred maintenance. The East Winds Bar still occupies the building in the left background.

John Fuller photo

Figure 4.39 (*Right*) At Belt Crossing on the southeast side of Indianapolis, a Big Four/New York Central passenger train is about to hit the "diamonds" (the railroad term for the pattern formed by the tracks at the crossing). The photo is undated and the train's direction is not noted. An educated guess is that it's the mid-1950s and the train is eastbound toward Cincinnati.

Jay Williams photo

Figure 4.40 (*Left*) DX Tower controlled the crossing of the Big Four main line and the Belt's LE&W extension. This valuation photo looks north. The huge smokestacks serve a factory behind the tower.

ICC valuation photo,
Richard K. Baldwin collection

Figure 4.41 (*Facing*) By the summer of 1961 DX had been altered a little, and the Belt's colorful caboose fleet was still in use. The westbound transfer run has interchange cars for the Nickel Plate.

Jay Williams photo

Figure 4.42 A southward view from 1912 shows the elegant entrance gate at the stockyards. Note the track and trolley wire passing through the arch at the right. Indianapolis Railways had a streetcar line that turned around on a loop deep in the yards.

Indiana Historical Society, Bass Photo Co. Collection

Rule #37 required that "trains must be run with the greatest of care and under control at all times, expecting to find tracks occupied by other trains or cars, and in going around curves, or at other places where the engineman's view of the track is obstructed, he must require the fireman or other trainmen on engine to keep necessary lookout." Other rules required that trains could move only on signal from tower operators, signalmen, or switch tenders, all of whom had sole responsibility for lining up routes as instructed by the dispatcher located in a facility at Harding Street on the city's west side, and later in the Conrail building near Union Station on Georgia Street (where CSX Transportation has facilities today).

For a railroad operating under the oldest of traffic control systems—hand signals from people on the ground, with train separation almost entirely on the basis of visual cues—the Belt seems to have run with surprising efficiency. In 1920, for example, freight cars handled in both tenants' and Belt trains totaled just over 1,350,000, or 3,700 every day—the equivalent of nearly seventy-five fifty-car trains, an average of one about every twenty minutes around the clock. By 1941 the car count was nearly two million, all handled on the same physical plant as in the 1920s.[25]

The Stockyards

The stockyards were a major Indianapolis business for the final quarter of the nineteenth century and for nearly seven decades of the twentieth, and the company paused in the fall of 1927 to look back and celebrate its accomplishments. The *Indianapolis Star* printed a special tabloid "Stock Yards Section" on November 11, 1927,[26] noting that the yards began on an eight-acre site but a half century later occupied 150 acres, almost a quarter of a square mile, and that the stockyards were the fifth largest in the country. The tabloid contained history, photos past and present, and ads placed by the Live Stock Exchange, the Kingan Company, Brown Brothers Beef and Pork Packers, truck manufacturers and dealers, a cattle company, banks, and the Hartford Transit Live Stock Insurance Company. The published statistics were impressive; for example, the fact that more than 104,850,000 head

THE BELT R R & STOCK YARDS COMPANY

179

Figure 4.43 The ebb and flow of porkers like these, among other livestock, were the currency of the stockyards over the facility's nine-decade life.

Indiana Historical Society, Bass Photo Co. Collection

of livestock had been received and shipped over fifty years. There was a huge barbecue for those attending,[27] and the stockyards tabloid even recounted a "furore" arising from the arrival of a 180-pound Duroc Jersey hog by airplane, apparently for the first time in aviation history.

Forty more years of prosperity were in store for the stockyards, but as time went on and both truck technology and highway construction converged, the Belt Railroad and its connections began to lose livestock traffic. In 1940 the company reported that 100 percent of receipts of livestock and 60 percent of outgoing stock went by truck.[28] This left only a small amount of total stockyards traffic for the railroads, and even that would continue to decline.

The Belt Railroad and Stock Yard Company had resolved in April of 1939 that it would no longer operate a railroad but would continue to have the power to own and lease a railroad, deal in real and personal property, and operate and maintain a public stockyard.[29] Indianapolis Stockyards Company, Inc., continued to operate the stockyards in the post–World War II era and into the 1960s. Then, in what seemed an abrupt and even unexpected action, the board of directors voted in 1967 to dissolve the company after selling the stockyards property to Eli Lilly and Company. Lilly then built its industrial center on the stockyards land and on adjacent property between Harding Street and White River Parkway. However, even though the Stockyards Company had not operated the Belt since 1939 and largely ignored it over the years, it still legally owned the railroad (remember that it was only leased to and not owned by the Indianapolis Union Railway). This ownership transferred with the stockyards property to Lilly, which today owns the Belt, leases it to CSX, and ships on it.

NOTES

1. When it came to interchange of cars among various lines, the principal bogeyman of the early railroad era was the often wide difference in track gauge. This could range from 4'8.5" between the rails ("standard gauge") to 4'10"; 5'; 5'4"; 5'6"; and 6'. Some were built to "narrow" gauge, defined as anything less than "standard." Often done to discourage connections between lines and thereby keep traffic tied to a particular line, this ultimately resulted in the need for expensive conversions when standard gauge indeed became the standard. In Indianapolis this was apparently only a minor problem because specially equipped cars could navigate both the standard-gauge tracks of most of the city's railroads and the inch-and-a-half wider gauge of some lines that ran into Ohio. Early interconnection of all the city's rail lines was the salubrious result. See George Rogers Taylor and Irene D. Neu, *The American Railroad Network, 1861–1890* (Urbana: University of Illinois Press, 2003). Originally published in 1956 by Harvard University Press, this volume is a very thorough treatment of the early railroad gauge problem.

2. Luther R. Martin, Real State Broker, *Map of Indianapolis*, 1870. Original in the collections of the Indiana State Library, I Map S 912.772 IMaI 70m (1870).

3. Robert G. Lewis, *Handbook of American Railroads* (New York: Simmons-Boardman Publishing, 1951), 91.

4. Association of American Railroads, *Quiz on Railroads and Railroading* (Washington, DC, 1947), questions 346 and 347, n.p.

5. *1877 The Belt Railroad and Stock Yards Company 1927 Golden Jubilee*, typescript, no author. This document appears to have been reprinted in its entirety in a special "Stock Yards Section" tabloid of the *Indianapolis Star* celebrating the fiftieth anniversary of the stockyards, November 11, 1927. It apparently was provided by the stockyards company to the newspaper for publication in the special section.

6. Jacob P. Dunn, *Greater Indianapolis* (Chicago: Lewis Publishing Co., 1910), quoted in Simons and Parker, *Railroads of Indiana*, 199.

7. *Articles of Association of the Indianapolis Belt Railway Company*. Photocopy of typescript, Indiana Historical Society, Collection #M67, Box 1, Folder 1.

8. Berry R. Sulgrove, *History of Indianapolis and Marion County, Indiana* (Philadelphia: L. H. Everts & Co., 1884), 136.

9. Manuscript in William Henry Smith Memorial Library, Indiana Historical Society, collection #s M 0067, BV 0672–0712, Box 1: Indianapolis Belt and Stock Yards Company Records, 1874–1968.

10. Robert V. Bruce, *1877: Year of Violence* (Indianapolis, IN: New Bobbs-Merrill Company, 1959), 288.

11. S. W. Durant, Civil Engineer, *Plan of Indianapolis* (St. Charles, IL, 1876).

12. William B. Burford, *R. L. Polk & Co's City Directory Map of Indianapolis, Ind.*, 1889.

13. *Report of the Board of Directors, Office of the Union Railroad, Transfer & Stock Yard Company*. Indianapolis, February 4, 1879. This document is in the collections of the William Henry Smith Memorial Library, Indiana Historical Society.

14. Richard T. Wallis, *The Pennsylvania Railroad at Bay* (Bloomington: Indiana University Press, 2001), 61. This comprehensive, detailed business history of the Terre Haute & Indianapolis Railroad Company (a descendant of the Terre Haute & Richmond Railroad) and its fractious relationship with the "Pennsy" provides fascinating insight into the complexities of railroad finance, management, and operation in post–Civil War Indiana.

15. 1879 annual report, Union Railroad, Transfer and Stock Yard Company.

16. Association of American Railroads, *Quiz on Railroads and Railroading* (Washington, DC, 1947).

17. Summaries of the evolution of the companies associated with the Belt are taken from volume 4 of *Corporate History of the Pennsylvania Lines West of Pittsburgh, Series, A*, 1899.

18. "Sta." means "station," but not in the railroad sense of a named location or a depot. The term is used by engineers and others to refer to distance measurements in segments of 100 feet. If the starting point is "Station 0+00," for example, a point 100 feet from that starting point is "Station 1+00." This provides a more precise means of measurement than using, for example, miles and fractions of miles. "M.P." in the report means "milepost," a physical marker labeled with the mileage from a given starting point on a railroad. The ICC report translated its station numbers into milepost numbers because railroaders were more used to using the latter to measure distances.

19. Railroad Community Committee of Indianapolis, *The Belt Railroad–Industrial Lifeline of Indianapolis*, 1956, n.p.

20. For those unfamiliar with the Whyte system of locomotive classification, it refers to the number of unpowered leading wheels, then the number of driving wheels, and finally the number of unpowered trailing wheels of a steam engine. An 0–6–0, then, would have no leading or trailing wheels and six driving wheels. This type of locomotive, along with the 0–8–0 and on some railroads the 0–10–0 wheel arrangement, was well suited for slow-speed movement of heavy trains and for switching work on a railroad such as the Belt because all the locomotive's weight was on the driving wheels.

21. Most information on the IU steam fleet was on an unnumbered loose sheet from the ICC valuation records, courtesy of collector Brian Banta.

22. Information on IU diesel locomotives came from a very thorough article on the Indianapolis Union Railway's locomotives in *Diesel Era* 15, no. 2 (March/April 2004): 45–51.

23. "Rules and Regulations," Office of the Indianapolis Union Railway Co., January 1, 1891, single-page printed sheet. Collection of Richard K. Baldwin.

24. Indianapolis Union Railway Company, *Rules Governing Employes [sic] of the Indianapolis Union Railway Co. and Employes of Other Companies When Using Belt Railroad and Union Tracks*, February 1, 1910, 19. For those unfamiliar with railroad practices, any trains not identified in and operating according to schedules in official timetables are called "extras" and may be operated at any time. Classification signals are colored lights or flags carried at the head of a locomotive indicating whether a train is an extra or a second section of a preceding scheduled train. On the Belt the locomotive number and the initials of the railroad operating it were used as unique identifiers in moving trains over the railroad. This avoided confusion that could result from locomotives of different railroads having the same number.

25. These figures are from annual reports of the Indianapolis Union Railway Company in the holdings of the William Henry Smith Memorial Library, Indiana Historical Society.

26. *Indianapolis Star*, "Stock Yards Section," November 11, 1927, 12. William Henry Smith Memorial Library, Indiana Historical Society, Indianapolis Belt Railroad and Stockyard Company records, Box 1, Folder 9.

27. It was quite a barbecue, catered by the Broad Ripple Beach and Zoo: among the catered items were two 600-pound beeves, two 200-pound hogs,

350 pounds of ham, 5,000 buns, 60 pounds of coffee, and 100 pounds of sugar. Deleted from the catering list were 100 pounds of cabbage and "10 gallons beef blood." Letter dated September 20, 1927, from Broad Ripple Beach and Zoo to S. E. Rauh, Indianapolis Stockyards.

28. William Henry Smith Memorial Library, Indiana Historical Society library, Collection #s M 0067, BV 0672–0712, Box 1: Indianapolis Belt and Stock Yards Company Records, 1874–1968.

29. Ibid., 16.

5

THE CITY AND ITS RAILROADS

W. R. HOLLOWAY'S HISTORY described the railroad as spurring Indianapolis to mature, causing "a change of features, of form, a suggestion of manhood, a trace of the beard, . . . of virility. . . . Everyone felt the impulse . . . of prosperity."[1] He was right, if a bit florid: urban maturity meant having railroad service. And for larger cities with multiple rail lines, the real rite of passage was a union station, a gateway to the city, a stepping-stone to prosperity; it gave travelers their first impression of a city and shaped its public image.

The two union stations of Indianapolis did just that: they spoke for the city through their stylistic designs, their large scale, and the quality of their materials. Differing greatly in size and appearance, each was right for its time. Each lent a sense of decorum to rail travel and communicated the prosperity, permanence, and good business sense of both the railroad companies and the city.

Railroads both attracted and repelled urban development. Most people did not desire life by a railroad, but many businesses did. In Indianapolis the narrow corridor of the Union Tracks reduced the railroads' negative impacts on the city at large while stimulating commercial and industrial activity in the immediate vicinity. Homes, schools, churches, and public institutions did not locate there, but hotels, wholesale houses, retail stores, and warehouses did. Many buildings that housed such businesses remain around Union Station today in the historic Wholesale District, evidence of the positive economic effect of the railroad. In addition, the two depots were destinations in themselves, particularly the 1888 depot. Restaurants, restrooms, newsstands, telegraph and telephone services, and barber services made the depots part of the city's daily life.

This book does not discuss the streetcars and interurbans of Indianapolis. Interurbans siphoned off considerable local traffic from the steam railroads, although none of the steam roads lost passenger service entirely until the Depression, by which time the interurbans had begun their final decline. The electric lines were important to both Indianapolis and Indiana, providing frequent service to most major cities in the state's northern half and stimulating early suburban development, growth of rural areas, and electrification of cities and villages. Indiana was the nexus of the early-twentieth-century "Interurban Era" and Indianapolis was the jewel in the crown, hosting some thirteen interurban routes, more than any other American city; it also had the nation's largest interurban traction terminal, built in 1904. Like Union Station, it stimulated nearby commercial development. Streetcars, in turn, inspired growth of "streetcar suburbs" that enabled downtown workers to live well outside the downtown area.

These electrified railroads had a different impact on central Indianapolis than the steam roads, for one main reason: they ran mainly in city streets. They typically did not occupy large, linear tracts of land devoted exclusively to railroad use, and they were built after the physical setting into which they were introduced was largely in place. Useful though they were in their time, they were an overlay on an existing urban form, and by their nature they had much less physical impact than did comparable steam railroad mileage. Streetcars did trigger extension of the street grid and help enlarge the city's footprint, but they did little to alter its physical character. Steam railroads, by contrast, often were boundaries or barriers rather than an integral part of the streetscape (think of the pejorative "the other side of the tracks," which was not a reference to streetcar tracks) and had a much greater impact on urban form and character than did the streetcars and interurbans.

Sixteen railroad lines converged upon Indianapolis between 1847 and 1918. Much of this network was in place by 1870, and it is clear that the nearly eighteenfold increase in the city's population between 1840 and 1870 (from 2,692 citizens to 48,244)[2] was due to the railroads, not because Indiana's roads had suddenly become better.

Railroad corridors varied in width and depth depending on the enterprises attracted to them: a rail-served warehouse might be half a block or less in size, while, in Indianapolis, for example, the Citizens Gas and Coke utility or the west side General Motors plant took up many acres and extended well back from the railroad. Rail corridors tended to be consistently commercial or industrial in character, with few residential, park, playground, or institutional land uses, and this affected the feeling, character, and appearance of a city. Furthermore, the types of industry drawn to the railroad affected nearby development patterns: a coke plant, for example, was a much more noxious neighbor than a warehouse and would discourage nearby development. These influences are visible today in the commercial character along the former Union Tracks—in the mile-and-a-quarter downtown elevated rail line that runs by Union Station and in the strongly industrial character along the former Indianapolis Belt.

Twentieth-Century Challenges
Changes on the Indianapolis Belt Railroad

Originally surrounded by vacant land, the Belt spurred development of a crescent-shaped industrial corridor along its main line. The tenant railroads built interchange yards adjacent to the Belt, extending its impact on the landscape out beyond its track. At its peak, the Belt was almost entirely double-tracked, with long stretches of quadruple track; it had many sidings and spurs, operators' towers at every railroad crossing, and switchmen's and crossing guard shanties at critical points and highway grade crossings. It employed more than four hundred workers.

It prospered for many decades but in time came to have less and less physical plant. Forces beyond its control brought lower traffic levels, reductions in trackage, closing of towers and shanties, and fewer employees. This resulted from the moving or closing of lineside industries; a switch to highway shipping; changes in dispatching, safety technology, and traffic control; and construction of the Big Four Yard (also called Avon Yard) west of downtown Indianapolis in 1960. This New York Central yard consolidated classification (car-sorting) work and caused the downgrading or closing of several Belt-served yards. This accelerated after the 1968 New York Central–Pennsylvania merger, when Avon became Penn Central's primary Indianapolis yard.

The Union Railway leased the Belt in the early 1880s and kept the two railroads' accounts separately. It never issued capital stock, but in 1913 it did issue ownership certificates to successors of its original organizers. The Pan Handle/Pennsylvania Railroad received three certificates, each representing a one-fifth share of ownership, and the Big Four/New York Central Railroad received two such certificates.[3] This ratio did not reflect traffic levels or the number of routes but rather the ownership interests of the original creators of the Belt in the 1870s (three were PRR predecessors and two were NYC). The remaining four railroads serving the city in 1913—the Baltimore & Ohio, the Nickel Plate, the Illinois Central, and the Monon—remained non-owning tenants, but no one railroad was favored over any other, costs were shared based on traffic levels, and all six railroads had equal rights to Union and Belt tracks and facilities.

In 1968 the Belt became a Penn Central (PC) property but, even as PC's prospects dimmed, the Belt's physical plant remained much as it had been decades earlier, though annual reports noted declining revenues compared to the 1950s and 1960s. Some industrial spurs had disappeared, as had enterprises such as small coal yards, but main tracks and sidings remained largely intact and carried a fair amount of traffic. Some through traffic had been diverted to the Union Station bypass tracks; still, a 1977 Conrail map shows intact connections to all the rail routes intersecting the Belt.

The Staggers Rail Act of 1980, named for its West Virginia sponsor in Congress, eliminated much federal regulation of freight railroads and permitted competitive rates, abandonment of low-value track, and transfer of track to regional and short line railroads. Through enlightened regulation, creative railroad management, and hardworking employees the rail industry of the twenty-first century emerged. By this time, though, the Belt had too much track and too few customers. "Rationalization" was inevitable, and by the late 1990s it had become the "IU Belt Running Track," a long single-track freight spur, no longer a discrete railroad—just a small part of a bigger one. But important customers remained, including a lubrications company, a recycling plant, and the Indianapolis Water Company at the west end; Central Soya above 18th Street; Evans Milling below West 10th Street; Carter Lee Lumber; the General Motors Metal Fabricating Division plant; the Eli Lilly plant on the site of the old stockyards; National Starch west of White River Bridge #2; Rykoff-Sexton Foods along Churchman Avenue; General Aluminum and Chemical Company and Interstate Warehouse along Keystone Avenue; the Indianapolis Coke/Citizens Gas & Coke plant between mileposts 8 and 9; Max Katz Bag Company;

The Indianapolis Union Railway Co.

Form 400 6-66   **Station Numbers—Belt Railroad**

No.	Customer
3	O. Martin Coal Co.
4	Ready Mixed Concrete Corporation
5	Cinder Block & Material Company
7	
8	American Block Co., Incorporated; M. Ross Masson Co.; Harris Barriers, Inc.
12	Bryant Div. of Carrier Corporation
13	Peanut Products Co.; Indiana Vinegar Co.
16	Central Soya Co. Chemurgy Div.
18	Indiana Equipment Co., Incorporated
21	Indianapolis Water Company; General Electric Supply Co.; Hotpoint Appliance Sales Co.; Westinghouse Electric Supply Co.; Radio Equipment Co.; C. P. Lesh Paper Co.
22	Indianapolis Water Co.
23	Behr Manning Corp.
24	Goodyear Tire & Rubber Co., Inc.; Carson, Pirie, Scott & Company; Anderson Storm Window & Door Co.
25	
36	Evans Milling Co.
37	Baker-McHenry & Welch, Inc.; Edw. Hines Lumber Company
43	General Electric Co.
44	Keystone Distributors
45	Sam Wolkoff & Co.
60	P. & E.
61	B. & O. (West)
65	Carter Lee Lumber Co.
67	Carter Lee Lumber Co.
68	American Fabricating Company
70	Merz Engineering Inc.
71	N. Y. C. R. R. (St. Louis Div.)
72	Pennsylvania (St. Louis Div.)
73	Chevrolet-Indianapolis
74	Ansted Corporation
75	American Bearing Corporation; Magnus Bearing Div. of National Lead Co.
76	Railway Service & Supply Co.
77	Equipment Rentals Corp.; Standard Dry Kiln Co.
78	Lee Sash & Door Co.; Allis Chalmers Mfg. Co.
84	Harding Iron Co.
85	Thiesing Veneer Co.; Standard Auto Parts & Tire Co.
86	Liquid Carbonic Div., Gen. Dynamics
87	Dependable Coal Co.
88	Ochs Paper Co.; Small & Schelosky Co.
89	Maurice Perk Metal Products
92	Best Foods, Inc.
94	Union Stock Yards (Live St.)
100	Union Stock Yards; Indianapolis Stock Yards Co., Inc.; Wright Bachman Inc.
102	Pennsylvania (Indpls. Div.)
104	Wright Bachman Inc.; Nutrena Mills, Inc.; Central Indiana Supply Co.
105	Belt Railroad Shops
106	International Minerals & Chem. Corp.
107	Stewart Warner Corp.
108	Marion Mfg. Co.
115	National Starch & Chem. Corporation
116	Cleveland Wrecking Co.; Stark-Wetzel & Co., Inc.
118	American Aggregates Corporation; Ready Mixed Concrete Corporation
120	Illinois Central
124	Indpls. Mach. & Supply Co.
129	Indpls. Ice & Fuel Co.
132	Indpls. Ice & Fuel Co.
133	American Can Co.
134	South Side Ice Co.
135	Pennsylvania (Louisville Div.)
140	Central States Bridge & Structural Co.
144	
145	
146	Bemis Bros. Bag Co.
151	Gulf Oil Corp.
153	Co-op Warehousing, Inc.
155	American Box. Co.
156	International Metal Polish Co.
157	J. I. Holcomb Mfg. Co.; Holcomb & Hoke Mfg. Co.
163	Industrial Salvage Corp.
165	Chrysler Corp.
170	John Sexton & Co.
175	
176	Indpls. Transit Mix
178	N. Y. C. R. R. (Cinn. Div.)
179	Indiana Excelsior Co.
180	Fairmount Glass Works, Inc.
182	N. Y. C. R. R. (Chicago Div.)
184	Ice House
186	Citizens Gas & Coke Utility
188	Pennsylvania-Hawthorne Yard (East Y)
189	Trans City Terminal Warehouse
190	P. R. Mallory & Co., Inc.
191	B. & O. (East)
192	Pennsylvania-Hawthorne Yard (West Y)
194	Potter Coal & Material Company
195	Pennsylvania (LaSalle St.)
198	Sears Roebuck & Co.
205	Ernest Johnson Coal Co.
209	Blakley Granite Co.
211	Thompson-Hayward Chem. Co.
212	RCA Victor Div. of Radio Corp. of America
213	RCA Victor Div. of Radio Corp. of America
214	Insley Mfg. Co.
216	
220	Ready Mixed Concrete Co.
223	Curry Miller Veneers, Inc.
225	John J. Madden Mfg. Co.
235	Marietta Mfg. Co.; U. S. Envelope Co.; Richardson Co.; Jack Hicks & Assoc.; Kavanaugh Supply Co.; Brightwood Transfer Company
239	N. Y. C. R. R. (P. & E. East Jct.)
243	Interstate Lumber & Hardware Co.
245	Interstate Foundry Co., Incorporated
250	N. Y. C. R. R. (Cleveland Div.)
271	Fuller Halpin Lumber Co., Incorporated
272	MacAllister Machinery Co., Inc.
275	Veline Co., Inc.
281	Hoosier Veneer Co.
288	L. S. Ayres & Co.
290	Lilly Paint Products Incorporated; The Dorrell Co.
294	Lincoln Fuel Co.
301	Central Veneer Co.
309	Ermet Products Co.; Indianapolis Ice & Fuel Co.
314	L. S. Ayres & Co.
316	Mobile Oil Co.
317	National Lead Co.
319	Baxter Steel Equip. Co.
327	Carlsen Concrete Supply Company
328	Trans City Warehouse
329	Norfolk & Western Ry.
330	Monon R. R.

Station Numbers—Union Tracks

No.	Track/Customer
390	West Line West Street
391	Pennsylvania Conn. Kentucky Ave.
392	P. & E. Conn. West Street
400	
401	N. Y. C. R. R. (Old Chicago Div.); Food Specialties, Inc.
404	Kittles, Inc.
405	Crescent Paper Co.; Georgia Street Realty Co.; Shaw-Walker Co.; Ferger Flour Co.; Diamond Chain Co., Inc.
406	Allison Coupon Co.
407	Capital Avenue Coach Yards
408	West End Union Station (West Line Capital Avenue)
410	Illinois Central Conn. Senate Avenue
414	N. Y. C. R. R. (P. & E. Tenn. St. Yd.)
415	Rolling Mill Track
421	Center Line Un. Sta. (Center of Concourse)
428	Pennsylvania Conn. West Y. (South St.)
429	East End Un. Sta. (East Line Meridian St.)
430	Indiana Terminal & Rfg. Co.
431	I. U. Storage Track
435	Pennsylvania East Y (South St.)
436	N. Y. C. R. R. Freight House Connection
438	Pennsylvania Conn. Davidson St.
439	B. & O. Conn. Davidson St.
440	Pennsylvania Conn. College Ave.
441	N. Y. C. R. R. Conn. College Ave.
443	Standard Grocery Co.
444	N. Y. C. R. R. Conn. Park Ave.
446	Monon R.R. Conn. Park Ave.
447	Center East Washington St.

Figure 5.1 (*Left*) For a small railroad, especially as late as 1966, the Belt had a lot of stations. Just as "switch" numbers identified specific pieces of track, station numbers indicated both specific points on the railroad and various customers; there were plenty of both.

Richard K. Baldwin collection

Figure 5.2 (*Facing*) South and east of Union Station, the Pennsylvania Railroad once had large freight houses along its Louisville line, on the site of the depot of the pioneer Madison & Indianapolis Railroad. As customers, freight traffic, and transportation technology changed, such buildings disappeared from all the city's railroads.

Indiana Historical Society, Bass Photo Co. Collection

215217-F

PENNSYLVANIA RAILROAD
OUT-BOUND FREIGHT HOUSE

Thomson Consumer Electronics (RCA) at milepost 10; and the Conner Corporation and Central States Warehouse on the former LE&W Extension.

The Indianapolis Union Railway, including the Belt, was absorbed by Conrail on February 1, 1977, and most of Conrail was divided between CSX and Norfolk Southern (NS) in 1999, making Indianapolis almost entirely a CSX town. Since then the Belt's tracks and customers have been further reduced, but it remains part of the Indianapolis railroad scene.

Changes on the Indianapolis Union Railway

The fate of Union Station and the Union Tracks was linked to that of the passenger train. The decline of rail travel over the half century preceding 1971 resulted from the nation's rise as an industrial power and the resulting revolution in transportation technology. The simple story is that people rode trains until they found another way to get around: the mass-produced and affordable automobile. Coupled with public highway funding, this increasingly affected both passenger and freight trains by facilitating private car use and bus and truck transportation. More and more passengers, mail, express, and high-value freight left the railroads, and the Depression dealt a further blow despite the introduction of innovative lightweight "streamliners" on some railroads.

World War II then brought travel demand to an unprecedented peak. A 1945 Pennsylvania Railroad timetable noted that train travel was four times what it had been in 1939, spurred by halted auto production, tire and gasoline rationing, and movement of nearly all military freight and passenger traffic by rail.

The railroads concluded, perhaps reasonably at the time, that there had been a rebirth. With the arrival of modern postwar trains, passenger counts indeed were buoyed, but the downturn resumed by the early 1950s as auto production rose, highways were paved, and air travel grew. Passenger trains were increasingly unprofitable, and, unwilling or unable to cover losses from freight revenues, and lacking public funding enjoyed by competing modes, railroads filed a stream of train-off petitions (applications to state authorities or the Interstate Commerce Commission to discontinue specific trains). By the late 1960s, disappearance of the passenger train was nigh. In response, Congress in 1970 created Amtrak (officially the National Railroad Passenger Corporation) to preserve a national network but with the assumption that trains would run for a while until they died a natural death. Despite this cynical start, decades of inadequate funding, and constant attacks on its life, Amtrak forgot to die and today has broad public support even though its skeletal network is a faint echo of what the nation once had.

All Indianapolis railroad routes had passenger service until the first discontinuances early in the Depression. The New York Central operated six routes and the Pennsylvania five; these had the greatest train density. The Baltimore & Ohio, the Illinois Central, the Monon, and the Nickel Plate operated the final five routes, the B&O running two of them; all used Union Station. Of these four, the Nickel Plate quit first, its last Michigan City trains running in 1932. Next was Illinois Central's Effingham, Illinois, service, stopped under a 1945 federal order to discontinue "lightly-patronized trains" to release cars to the military. The Baltimore & Ohio between Springfield, Illinois, and Hamilton,

The decline of the passenger train is a sorry tale, but the railroads did try to keep the public riding the rails. Passenger railcar purchases after World War II showed that they expected and wanted to provide high-quality service. Despite competition from autos, buses, and airlines, the railroads thought that amenity-rich modern cars, a new level of comfort, and convenient scheduling would enable trains to hold their own. The Pennsylvania and the New York Central bought coaches, diners, lounges, sleepers, and observation cars, dubbing them, respectively, "the Blue Ribbon Fleet" and "the Great Steel Fleet." Situated astride major routes of both railroads, Indianapolis enjoyed these upgraded services. The New York Central in the summer of 1949 ran nine daily trains—four eastbound and five westbound—through Indianapolis on just the run between Cleveland and St. Louis. On the Pennsylvania, seven trains in each direction served the New York–St. Louis route. In the *Official Guide* the New York Central had nine pages describing the cars in all of its trains and forty-eight pages of passenger timetables; the Pennsylvania had sixteen pages of car descriptions and seventy pages of timetables.

But it was a great effort doomed to fail. In addition to highway and air competition, the railroads steadily lost mail revenue as the U.S. Post Office moved from rail to truck and air. The abrupt cancellation of nearly every railroad mail contract in 1967 was the final blow that made Amtrak inevitable.

Figure 5.3 Even as late as 1968, in Penn Central days, Union Station hosted some substantial trains. The *South Wind*, running between Chicago and Florida, was one.

Jay Williams photo

Ohio, via Indianapolis had lost its trains by 1950, and even Indiana's own, the Monon, dropped its Chicago–Indianapolis service in 1959.[4] Then only the New York Central and the Pennsylvania, combined as Penn Central in 1968, still had service. PC soon coasted into bankruptcy, so, in Indianapolis anyway, this was not the passenger train's finest hour.

Of the Pennsylvania's five routes—Chicago–Indianapolis and Indianapolis–Louisville (part of the Chicago–Florida route); Richmond–Indianapolis and Indianapolis–Terre Haute (part of the New York–St. Louis route); and the line to Vincennes—the last was the first to lose its trains, in 1931. The others retained service under Penn Central and for some time under Amtrak but are now gone.

New York Central's six routes were Cleveland–Indianapolis and Indianapolis–St. Louis; Chicago–Indianapolis and Indianapolis–Cincinnati; and the old Peoria & Eastern, Peoria–Indianapolis and Indianapolis–Columbus. The P&E had its modest service eliminated in stages by 1950 east of Indianapolis and 1957 west of the city; for many years it hosted shuttle trains between Union Station and the Indianapolis Motor Speedway. Service on the other NYC lines lasted through Penn Central until Amtrak,

except for the St. Louis line, which lost all service by the spring of 1968. East of Indianapolis, service on a Budd Rail Diesel Car continued between Indianapolis and Cleveland until the start of Amtrak. On the Chicago–Cincinnati line, the *James Whitcomb Riley* survived and continued for a while under Amtrak with the same name. The Riley Boosters Club worked hard to promote travel on this line as well as the PRR's Louisville line, which hosted the *South Wind* Florida service. Alas, this effort was too little and too late.

But all was not lost. On Amtrak's first day, May 1, 1971, the city still had service on five lines: Chicago–Indianapolis and Indianapolis–Cincinnati on the former NYC *Riley* route; the Indiana portion of the *National Limited* on the former PRR and on some former NYC track New York–Indianapolis and Indianapolis–Kansas City; and the Indianapolis–Louisville former PRR portion of the *South Wind* route to Florida (the *Riley* and the *South Wind* both used the former NYC route Chicago–Indianapolis). Over the next forty-plus years Amtrak's Indiana routes varied wildly, often missing Indianapolis entirely. Today the city has a blend of daily and thrice-weekly service: three times a week between Washington, DC, and Chicago on the *Cardinal*, and

Figure 5.4 Union Station could look deceptively busy late in the pre-Amtrak era. Here at the train shed's east end, four tracks are occupied with the comings and goings of Penn Central passenger and head-end traffic.

John Fuller collection

Figure 5.5 As passenger service shifted from Penn Central to Amtrak in 1971, Union Station hosted a few venerable veterans of better times.

John Fuller photo

service to Chicago the other four days on the *Hoosier State*. At this writing the latter train offers enhanced service levels on refurbished historic cars. This is on a trial basis, so its long-term fate has yet to be decided.

Imagine what this erosion of passenger rail service meant for Indianapolis Union Station in the decades following World War II. It could handle two hundred trains a day, but each discontinuance meant the station was emptier, gloomier, another order of magnitude too large for the remaining trains, increasingly uneconomical to keep operating when there was progressively less reason for it. It housed railroad offices and operations, but in time the old landmark outlived its usefulness even for that. Change came, too, to the Union Tracks up on the elevation, once a busy place incorporating the Union Station train shed, industrial spur tracks, a maze of switches east and west of the station, yard tracks for the Pullman Company and mail and express cars, approach tracks for the various railroads, the Pennsylvania Railroad Produce Yard, IU Tower to watch over the tracks east of Union Station, and an army of switch tenders, signalmen, maintenance crews, tower operators, depot personnel, and train crews. Much of this would disappear. In 1953 forty-three daily trains called at Union Station but only nineteen ten years later. During the Penn Central era it ran fourteen, and there were only six in Amtrak's early years.[5] Even so, the station tracks stayed largely intact into the Conrail era, which began April 1, 1976, when Penn Central and other northeastern bankrupts merged to attempt creation of a viable freight railroad—the Consolidated Rail Corporation, or Conrail for short—which, by the way, succeeded beyond all expectations. A 1977 Conrail map shows eight tracks in the Union

Station train shed, most of them unused. A little over twenty years later only tracks 9 and 10 remained for Amtrak trains; but all the trackless platforms were in place, too difficult to remove. The two freight bypass tracks south of the shed also remained. At the same time, rail-served businesses left downtown Indianapolis. As industrial spurs, the old Pullman coach yard, and other tracks and yards fell into disuse they were gradually torn up, leaving a lot of open space up on the elevation. With the reduction of passenger traffic, the bypass tracks became favored over the Belt as the main freight route through the city.

The Pennsylvania and the New York Central shared ownership of the Indianapolis Union Railway for fifty-five years, a period when the city's other four railroads dropped their passenger trains and stopped paying their share of Union Station's costs. Worsening finances meant that PRR, NYC, and then PC spent little on station maintenance, even though Amtrak relieved them of passenger train expenses and paid them to run trains and to use Union Station. PC went belly-up in June 1970, which meant an even lower priority for maintaining Victorian-era station buildings. There soon would follow a saga of nearly two decades' duration during which saving the station was always the goal but was never guaranteed.[6]

The bankrupt Penn Central, understandably, wanted to sell Union Station. A high demolition cost had kept the building standing, but that was no guarantee that someone would not buy it for its site. Various members of the community recognized the station's importance and, fortunately, so did the City of Indianapolis. In the summer of 1971, the city began purchase negotiations and then stepped out of the picture in favor of a private group,

Figure 5.6 This was the real story at Union Station in the late 1960s and early 1970s. Long periods of quiet were broken mostly by Penn Central freights passing the south side of the train shed rather than by the great passenger fleets that once called here.

John Fuller photo

Union Station Associates, that had real estate, construction, contracting, and architectural experience. The group bought the station for a little under $200,000 and raised more than twice that for critical repairs. Renovation planning and preliminary leasing moved forward, but the oil crisis, inflation, and economic slump of the early 1970s brought the effort to a standstill.

It became apparent that any effort to preserve Union Station would require a public-private partnership in which public financial support and a private developer would enable the city's

citizens to keep the old landmark as a part of their daily lives: everyone would help pay for it, and everyone would reap the benefit. Suburban development had long been supported by lavish subsidies in the form of new roads and freeways, extension of utilities, and tax breaks, but nothing close to that level of support had been offered to development in downtown areas other than the old urban renewal program that tore down far more than it built. In the mid-1970s, though, times were changing, and at least some leveling of the playing field was at hand.

Figures 5.7 and 5.8 (*Above and Facing*) By the summer of 1971 Indianapolis was suffering some ills shared with other major cities: way too much land devoted to surface parking, loss of much of its historic building stock, and an impressive railroad station hosting too few trains.

Jay Williams photos

Figure 5.9 Well into the Penn Central bankruptcy, the freight continued to move, if imperfectly. A 1973 view out the west end of the Union Station train shed shows an eastbound PC freight.

John Fuller photo

Figure 5.10 Having long outlived its usefulness, the coach yard northwest of the train shed was torn up in 1973; Union Station's prospects at this time seemed pretty dim, too.

John Fuller photo

Union Station Associates ended its efforts in 1977, and in 1978 the city did a study concluding that costs would be too high to convert the station to offices, which had seemed the most feasible use at the time. The city then began looking into federal funding. Fortunately, the flawed urban "renewal" idea—knock down the old stuff and developers will flock to the city to rebuild—had finally been recognized as the disaster it was. It was replaced by the Community Development Block Grant (CDBG) program, which gave cities much more leeway in how federal development funds were spent—allowing, among much else, investment in historic building preservation. Using some of its CDBG funds, the City of Indianapolis purchased Union Station in 1980. In that same year, Amtrak moved into a new facility, a depot under the train shed that it shared with intercity buses. A suitable use for the building itself, though, remained elusive.

Then fortunate timing again came into play. Union Station had been listed in the National Register of Historic Places in 1974. In 1981 Congress passed an economic recovery act that included significant tax credits for rehabilitation of National Register–listed buildings for income-producing uses. This made it economically feasible to put the station into a new use while carefully preserving its historic character. After rehabilitation by Robert Burns, a committed local developer, Union Station opened on April 26, 1986, as a festival marketplace similar to Quincy Market in Boston and South Street Seaport in New York. A new Holiday Inn hotel also was part of the development, utilizing a portion of the train shed.

In this new use, Union Station was a great success, triggering redevelopment of many of the surrounding buildings in the Wholesale District. However, over the next decade the festival marketplace model began to fade and business at the station went into a decline. Efforts to create a physical link between Union Station and the new Circle Centre shopping mall did not work out, and Union Station again ended up in the city's hands. The hotel, fortunately, still operated under Holiday Inn's Crowne Plaza brand and continued to do a good business, no doubt helped by the fact that it offered unique accommodations in renovated historic rail cars. The last of the festival marketplace tenants left Union Station early in 1997, and after a period of uncertainty, agreement was reached with the Crowne Plaza to operate the city-owned station as a banquet hall and conference center. The first event held there in this new use was a wedding, and since then many more people have come to various functions in this truly special place.

If one party can be given primary credit (and abundant thanks) for the rescue and the promising future of Union Station, it would be the City of Indianapolis. Yes, many in the community supported the station's preservation; developers took risks and spent money (and lost it, too, in the interest of keeping the building standing); and the Crowne Plaza has made a long-term commitment. By any measure this was a community preservation effort. But the City of Indianapolis is the one entity that has been there from the beginning, determined to keep trying to find the right mix of developers, users, and financing. It was not the city's job to save the building—its job was to facilitate Union Station's rescue in a way that made sense and that benefited the entire community. And that is what happened. Examples of this kind of municipal leadership are distressingly rare, and when they occur they should be celebrated.

Figure 5.11 In 1986, as the Union Station clock tower was receiving roof repairs during the building's renovation, the adjacent Hoosier Dome (later the RCA Dome) was two years old. Though built at a cost of more than $77 million, the domed (or perhaps doomed) stadium would not see its twenty-fifth birthday. Union Station turned 100 two years after this photo was taken. Is there a lesson here?

Jay Williams photo

Figures 5.12 and 5.13 (*Above and Facing*) The Union Station train shed serves three functions today: it provides a two-track bypass for freight trains through a new sheet metal enclosure along the shed's south side; Amtrak trains use tracks 9 and 10; and the area where tracks 1 through 7 once ran has been enclosed and finished as income-producing office space.

Author photos

Figure 5.14 East of Union Station, IU Tower still guards the Union Tracks, which are much reduced from earlier days. In the left foreground is the lead that splits into station tracks 9 and 10; the next two tracks are the freight bypass; and the Louisville line is in the background. The tracks continue farther east (to the left), where, out of the photo, former B&O and PRR routes, as well as the old Big Four Cincinnati line, diverge from the former Big Four Cleveland line.

Author photo

The Belt and the Union Today

The Belt

Most historic Indianapolis rail lines remain in place today, but not always as parts of the through routes they once were. Former New York Central lines, operated by CSX Transportation, have fared the best: the old Big Four Cleveland–St. Louis main (the "Indianapolis line" to the east and the "St. Louis line" to the west) is still double track and sees more traffic than any other line. The former Big Four Chicago–Cincinnati line is intact southeast of the city; CSX operates it to Shelbyville, and the Central Railroad Company of Indiana runs east of that point. The old Chicago line extends west of downtown and turns north at Brant; it is now the Zionsville Industrial Track and ends at about the north line of Marion County, making the storied route of the *Riley* an industrial branch. The former Peoria & Eastern's Peoria–Springfield, Ohio, line, which always had the least traffic, has been torn up between DX Tower, where it left the Big Four main, and Eastside Junction on the Belt but is intact east of the Belt as the Hunter Industrial Track (also called the 30th Street Runner), to industrial facilities beyond the east leg of I-465. West of downtown, the former P&E, which shared Big Four tracks, is intact to Brant, and then terminates at a west side tank farm. However, at CP Clermont, where the P&E and the former Indianapolis & Frankfort crossed, the P&E is intact westward to Crawfordsville, where it connects with the former Monon to Chicago. These segments host Amtrak's *Cardinal* and *Hoosier State*.

The Pennsylvania Railroad's former Pan Handle Pittsburgh–St. Louis route extends eastward as the Pine Runner and is abandoned east of Pine. West of downtown, the main line is in place to Davis but turns north there onto the former I&F to Frankfort. West of Davis, the former Pan Handle has been abandoned. The city's original railroad, the Madison & Indianapolis, which became the PRR's Louisville line, survives today as the Louisville & Indiana Railroad, operating on trackage rights from downtown to a point south of the Belt crossing at Dale. Finally, the former Indianapolis & Vincennes remains in operation as the Indiana Southern Railroad, although it no longer reaches Vincennes. It enters Indianapolis from the southwest, using trackage rights on CSX between Ray on the old I&V and CP Holt on the old Pan Handle via a connector called the Petersburg Secondary.

The Monon's Chicago line has been abandoned south of Monticello in White County; its right-of-way is now the eighteen-mile Monon Trail, which runs northward from the northeast side of downtown. The former LE&W/Nickel Plate/Norfolk & Western, which ran parallel to and east of the Monon, has been torn up from downtown north to 22nd Street. The Hoosier Heritage Port Authority owns the line up to Tipton; this is the route of passenger trains during the Indiana State Fair between Fishers and Gate 6 at the fairgrounds.

The former Baltimore & Ohio line to Hamilton, Ohio, runs east from the Union Tracks, turning slightly south a little beyond the Belt crossing at Pine. Part of CSX Transportation, it is the route of Amtrak's *Cardinal*, which, on its complicated route through Indiana and Illinois, runs on several historic fallen flag railroad routes. ("Fallen flag" refers to a railroad that either has been abandoned or has been absorbed into another, losing its

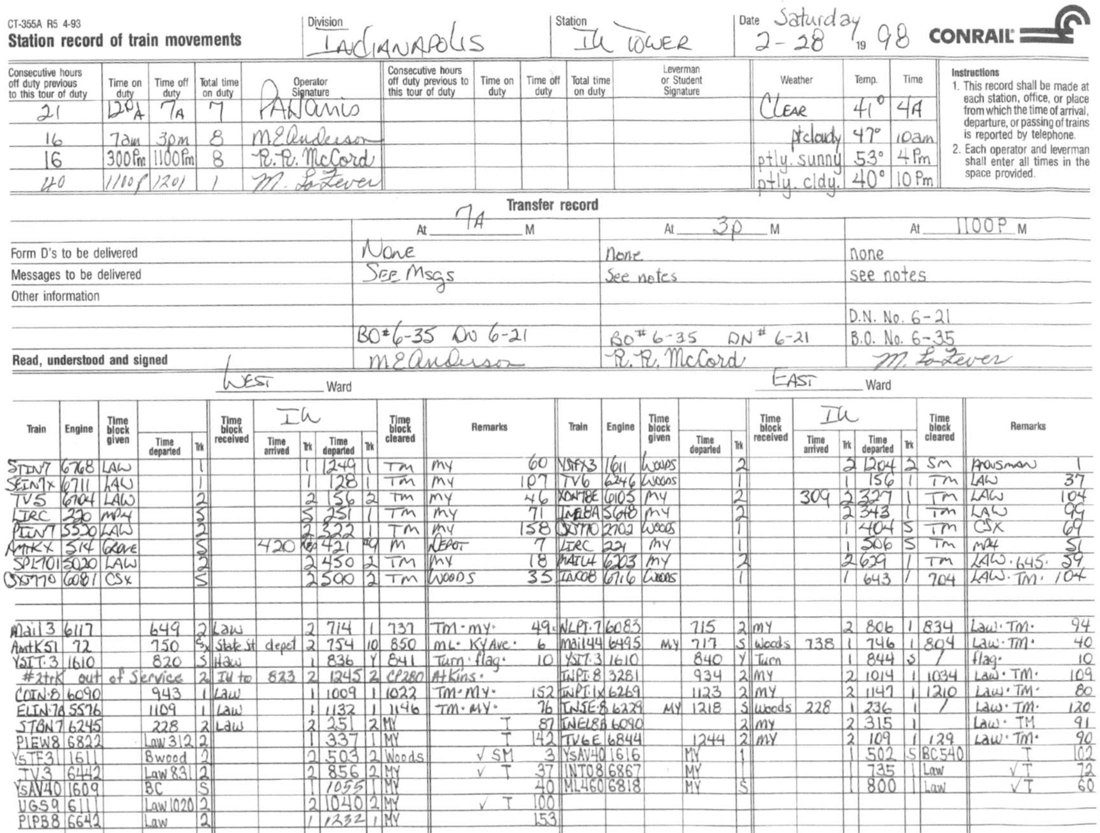

CT-355A R5 4-93
Station record of train movements
Division: Indianapolis | Station: IU Tower | Date: Saturday 2-28 19 98 | CONRAIL

Consecutive hours off duty previous to this tour of duty	Time on duty	Time off duty	Total time on duty	Operator Signature	Weather	Temp.	Time
21	12:01A	7A	7	P. Adams	Clear	41°	4A
16	7am	3pm	8	M. E. Anderson	ptcloudy	47°	10am
16	300Pm	1100Pm	8	R. R. McCord	ptly. sunny	53°	4Pm
20	1100P	1201	1	M. LeZever	ptly. cldy.	40°	10Pm

Instructions
1. This record shall be made at each station, office, or place from which the time of arrival, departure, or passing of trains is reported by telephone.
2. Each operator and leverman shall enter all times in the space provided.

Transfer record

	At 7A M	At 3P M	At 1100P M
Form D's to be delivered	None	None	none
Messages to be delivered	See Msgs	See notes	see notes
Other information			D.N. No. 6-21
	BO# 6-35 DN 6-21	BO# 6-35 DN# 6-21	B.O. No. 6-35
Read, understood and signed	M E Anderson	R. R. McCord	M. LeZever

West Ward — IU

Train	Engine	Time block given	Time departed	Trk	Time block received	Time arrived	Trk	Time departed	Trk	Time block cleared	Remarks
STIN7	6768	LAW		1			1	1249	1	TM	MY 60
SEIN7X	6711	LAW		1			1	128	1	TM	MY 107
TV5	6704	LAW		2			2	156	2	TM	MY 46
LIRC	220	MP4		S			S	251	1	TM	MY 71
PIIN7	5530	LAW		2			2	322	1	TM	MY 158
AMTK X	514	GROVE		S		420	Dep	421	#9	M	DEPOT 7
SPL701	5020	LAW		2			2	450	2	TM	MY 18
CSX770	6081	CSX		S			2	500	2	TM	WOODS 35
Mail 3	6117		649	2	Law		2	714	1	737	TM·MY· 49
AmtK51	72		750	Sx	State St	depot	2	754	10	850	ML· KY Ave· 6
YSIT·3	1610		820	S	Haw		1	836	Y	841	Turn·flag· 10
#2trK	out	of Service		2	IU to	823	2	1245	2	CP280	AtKins·
COIN·8	6090		943	1	Law		1	1009	1	1022	TM·MY· 152
ELIN·7A	5576		1109	1	Law		1	1132	1	1146	TM·MY· 76
STBN7	6245		228	2	Law		2	251	2	MY	T 87
PIEW8	6822		Law 312	2			1	337	1	MY	T 142
YSTF31	1611		Bwood	2			2	503	2	Woods	√ SM 3
TV3	6442		Law 831	2			2	856	2	MY	√ T 37
YSAV40	1609		BC	S			1	1055	1	MY	40
UGS9	6111		Law 1020	2			2	1040	2	MY	√ T 100
PIPB8	6642		Law	2			1	1232	1	MY	153

East Ward — IU

Train	Engine	Time block given	Time departed	Trk	Time block received	Time arrived	Trk	Time departed	Trk	Time block cleared	Remarks
NSIFX3	1611	Woods		2			2	1204	2	SM	Arousman 1
TV6	6246	Woods		1			1	156	1	TM	LAW 37
XDN78E	6105	MY		2		309	2	327	1	TM	LAW 104
INEL8A	5648	MY		2			2	343	1	TM	LAW 99
CSX770	2702	Woods		1			1	404	S	TM	CSX 69
LIRC	221	MY		1			1	506	S	TM	MP4 51
MAIL4	6203	MY		2			2	629	1	TM	LAW·645· 59
IACO8	6716	Woods		1			1	643	1	704	LAW·TM· 104
WLPT·7	6083		715	2	MY		2	806	1	834	Law·TM· 94
Mail44	6495	MY	717	S	Woods	738	1	746	1	804	Law·TM· 40
YSIT·3	1610		840	Y	Turn		1	844	S	/	flag· 10
INPI·8	3281		934	2	MY		2	1014	1	1034	Law·TM· 109
INPI·1X	6269		1123	2	MY		2	1147	1	1210	Law·TM· 80
INSE·8	6229	MY	1218	S	Woods	228	1	236	1	/	Law·TM· 120
INEL8B	6090			2	MY		2	315	1		Law·TM 91
TV6E	6844		1244	2	MY		2	109	1	129	Law·TM· 90
YSAV40	1616		MY	1			1	502	S	BC540	T 102
INTO8	6867		MY	1			1	735	1	Law	√ T 72
ML460	6818		MY	S			1	800	1	Law	√ T 60

Figure 5.15 A 1998 train sheet from IU recorded almost forty trains passing by the tower. There was a time when most if not all of them would have been routed around the Belt, but by this time that railroad had become just a long industrial track.

Courtesy of John Ricci

original or historic name and identity.) The former Illinois Central line shows how an obsolete railroad can be brought back to life. Operated since the mid-1980s by the Indiana Rail Road Company (INRD), this once-forlorn route has become a major regional freight railroad and a regular user of the Belt.

Fifth and last of the five "minor" Indianapolis railroad routes is the western portion of the Baltimore & Ohio, the line to Springfield, Illinois. This line diverged from the P&E at IJ, west of Union Station, and crossed the Belt at KD. Some track remains as part of the CSX line to Frankfort.

The Belt is reduced in size but still in service. The LE&W Extension has been torn up, and at the west end, track north of White River Bridge #1 and a small stub of the Big Four's old Chicago line are intact but unused, as is the Central Soya plant on this segment. The operating portion of the Belt is single track now and runs at ten miles per hour. Signals (mast and dwarf) still protect railroad crossings, and flashers operate at highway crossings, but interlocking towers, switchmen's and crossing guard shanties, and the Kentucky Avenue engine terminal all are gone. Connections to some railroads remain, but the Belt has been "rationalized" to the barest infrastructure enabling it to do its job. It serves industries such as Carter Lee Lumber, Cargill, Eli Lilly, Ingredion (formerly National Starch), and Max Katz Bag Company. CSX serves industries via the Belt on the old Peoria & Eastern line to Ohio. Other customers are gone, and much land to either side of the Belt is unused.

Even in its reduced state, the Belt sees daily service most of the time. Dispatched from CSX Great Lakes Division headquarters on Georgia Street, it runs on radio-, phone-, or electronically issued track warrants giving a train the exclusive right to operate within specified limits for a stated period of time. CSX serves online customers as needed but also uses the Belt as a bypass if the main at Union Station is out of service.

The Indiana Rail Road regularly uses Belt trackage rights from the Senate Avenue Yard connection. Because the connection is in the southeast quadrant of the grade-separated crossing, INRD trains back out of Senate Avenue and head up the connection onto the Belt. At Dale the train backs through the southeast connector and then proceeds north to IU and west past Union Station to Avon. Another route uses the Pine connector down to the former B&O and Pan Handle lines and then west through Union Station to Avon. INRD has trackage rights to Avon only for interchange and does not serve customers on the Belt. INRD trains receive track warrants on the Belt and then run on signal indication via IU to Avon. INRD also uses the Belt for interchange with Norfolk Southern at Hawthorne Yard, which the NS reaches by trackage rights from Anderson on CSX's Cleveland line.

There long have been plans to route trains around the city on the Belt and abandon the Indianapolis Union tracks. The elevation would be either removed or remade as an urban park like New York's High Line. This would be a major undertaking with significant implications for Indianapolis. What are the pros and cons? The track elevation served its purpose of separating railroad and city street traffic but has always been a barrier, a "blank wall." This term refers to any environmental element—a surface parking lot, windowless building wall, empty commercial storefront, bricked-up windows, freeway bridge or overpass—that creates a streetscape gap and discourages pedestrian traffic. The track elevation's height, length, and long, dark underpasses have made it a major blank wall that arguably has impeded commercial development to its south, where land use has been more diffuse and spotty, with more surface parking, vacant land, and a much less dense urban character than to the north.

Removing the track elevation would eliminate that blank wall and also make more land available for development, but what other effects would it have? One would be elimination of Amtrak's station under the train shed. Because intercity buses

Figure 5.16 The Belt still serves the Cargill grain plant on the west side at West Michigan and Cable streets. The main track diverges to the left of the plant switcher.

Author's collection

Figure 5.17 This view looks north along the Belt at Woods, where the former PRR/Pan Handle main crosses in the foreground. Not far beyond, the old NYC St. Louis main crosses the Belt at CP1; note the identifying sign on the junction's equipment shanty to the right of the crossing—at milepost 1 west of Indianapolis. New hooded mast signals apparently will replace the still-active dwarfs that protect the crossing at Woods but have not yet been powered up and turned to face the Belt track.

Author's collection

Figure 5.18 A northward view into the Indiana Rail Road's Senate
Avenue Yard shows a busy scene. The former Indianapolis Power
& Light plant is in the center background, with Lucas Oil Stadium
to the right. This was once Illinois Central Railroad trackage.

Author's collection

Figure 5.19 Old Pennsylvania Railroad position light signals still guard the Belt's crossing with the Louisville & Indiana Railroad, originally the pioneer Madison & Indianapolis. The view is north toward downtown Indianapolis, with the Belt crossing from left to right. The Belt/L&I connection diverges in the foreground.

Author's collection

Figure 5.20 Compare this view of Belt Crossing to the one in figure 4.39. The Belt and the Big Four today are both single track and lightly used. The view is northeast along the Belt, with remnants of the old coke plant in the background.

Author's collection

also use this facility, its closure would mean the loss of the city's only downtown bus/rail depot. There has been discussion of relocating Amtrak to the airport, which is technically feasible since the current Amtrak route passes close to the airport's north side. However, because access to the airport terminal building is from the west, a shuttle would be necessary between the rail and air terminals, and there is a question of how many travelers would connect between air and rail or be willing to make such an inconvenient connection. Furthermore, unless bus service also relocated here the benefits of an intermodal terminal would be lost. And, not least among considerations, removal of the station from the central city to a remote location discourages ridership. So the whole idea of relocating the Amtrak station becomes self-defeating unless it proceeds from the premise that rail and bus travel are not worth preserving and enhancing.

Then there is the issue of preserving Union Station. The depot itself is in no danger, but what about the train shed? It has been adapted to contain offices generating rental income, and the Crowne Plaza hotel is still there. Certainly the shed could be removed; Union Station could be modified and, with some new construction, the hotel facilities contained in the track elevation could be replaced. But the train shed is an integral part of the depot: the building would make little sense without it. Is this a course of action Indianapolis would even consider? And would it bear the cost involved?

The railroads using the elevation would, of course, be affected, too. Routing through freight traffic onto the IU tracks instead of the Belt has saved many train miles each day and avoids the many highway grade crossings along the Belt. Returning through traffic to the Belt is worth considering, but there are so many implications, with effects on so many disparate stakeholders, that balancing all these interests is a real challenge. One observer, however, has posed the most challenging question of all: This idea can work, but who is going to provide the half-billion dollars it will cost? Stay tuned.

The Union

The Indianapolis Union Railway, too, is less than it once was. It hosts daily freight and Amtrak trains but, except for Union Station, its train shed, and the track elevation structure, most of what existed on the IU at its peak in the 1920s has been swept away. It has a modest physical plant consisting of two main tracks, sidings leading to train shed tracks 9 and 10, and the wye to the Louisville line. The freight mains run on either side of IU Tower and then pass by the train shed in their own sheet-metal enclosure. Tracks west of Union Station once handled coal for the old Indianapolis Power and Light plant between West and Missouri streets,[7] but a recent switch to natural gas ended that traffic. IU Tower remains in place, but rumor has it that it faces demolition soon as a result of ongoing signaling and train control improvements. Overall, the elevation is doing its job but ties up a lot of urban land to do it. What to do with it is a true dilemma.

And Union Station? All who know it would agree that it embodies the qualities of good architecture articulated long ago by the Roman writer Vitruvius: firmness, commodity, and delight. It was built of solid and lasting materials, it performed its function well, and it is, today as in the past, a pleasure to behold.

So what about this landmark, a place unique in design and purpose, with a singular story to tell about the life of Indianapolis? The introduction of railroad transportation to American communities was an event of far-reaching significance that affected communities large and small.[8] Although he was writing about another city's Union Station, author Jeffrey Spivak captured the essence of how such a building can hold meaning for a city: "Yet, the building has come to mean so much more to its patrons, its city and its epoch. At its heart, Union Station was and remains a monumental embodiment of liberation, as much about linking places as about leaving them, as much about capping a confident age then as symbolizing an age of renewal today. As such, Union Station represents . . . a town bursting at the seams and full of big ideas, clamoring for a bigger station. . . . The citizenry embraced their monument, made it their town square and experienced magical moments there."[9]

The area around Union Station has seen dramatic change, most of it recent. Yet it still contains an important transportation corridor. It was always a convenient location for travelers and it remains so today. It is true, of course, that travelers can experience only the train shed of Union Station. The depot itself is no longer the rail gateway to the city. This has happened in many cities, the removal of depots from historic facilities too large and unwieldy for today's traffic levels. Sometimes the historic depot was demolished and a new one built on the same site: New York's Penn Station and Chicago Union Station are examples (though the latter's magnificent waiting room survives), or all of North Station and nearly all of South Station in Boston. In other cases (Kansas City, St. Louis, Pittsburgh), the historic depots survived and found new uses. There also are examples of historic depots serving their original purpose: Union Station in Portland, Oregon; Seattle's King Street Station; Los Angeles Union Passenger Terminal; and Denver Union Station.

Indianapolis Union Station is no longer a passenger depot, but it remains a vital part of the city and of the Crowne Plaza hotel. The hotel occupies part of the train shed, the station contains offices, and its public areas are a magnificent event venue. Up at track level, hotel guests stay in the renovated passenger cars parked on tracks along the original platforms. Much of the rest of the train shed contains office space, the rents from which help to keep the depot economically viable. Indeed, with all these changes of use, the depot, the train shed, and the concourse area beneath the shed survive remarkably intact, as does a good part of the structural system: in addition to being able to see the elevation's structural elements inside the Amtrak station, at platform level visitors can also view the train shed's graceful steel arches and what in its time was an innovative roof structure.

Over more than three decades, Union Station's prospects have risen and fallen and risen again until today, when it is rightfully revered as an essential part of Indianapolis, a shared possession of all its citizens, but not just a static remnant of the past. It serves a sound economic purpose, different from the purpose for which it was built but no less real. But Union Station also has value in a less tangible way, a way that cannot be measured in dollars and cents or bricks and mortar. In the prologue to his 2013 book *Grand Central*, author Sam Roberts wrote that "this book is more than a story about transportation. It's about the expansion of the city of New York into a metropolis and the aggregation of metropolitan government, which mirrored the ruthless consolidation of corporate America and of the nation's railroads. The terminal was a product of local politics, bold architecture, brutal flexing of corporate muscle, and visionary engineering. No other building embodies New York's ascent as vividly as Grand Central. And no other epitomizes the partnership that melded the best instincts of government with public-spirited private investment, a model that is being mirrored all over America."[10]

Yes, that model is indeed mirrored in Indianapolis. How fortunate we are to have such a landmark. Allowing for the differences in location, scale, players, and time period, did not this same story play out here in central Indiana as it did in New York City? Is it so far-fetched to propose that precisely the same dynamic has been at work in the Hoosier capital first to create and then to preserve a monumental work of architecture that, all on its own, embodies the story of a city?

NOTES

1. The Holloway passage is quoted in James R. Hetherington, "The History of Union Station," paper presented at the 2003 Railroad Symposium, Indiana Historical Society, archived at www.indianahistory.org, unpaginated.

2. David J. Bodenhamer and Robert G. Barrows, eds., *The Encyclopedia of Indianapolis* (Bloomington: Indiana University Press, 1994), 1480, 1482.

3. *Corporate History of the Pennsylvania Lines West of Pittsburg*, Series A, Volume 4, 1899, 460–1.

4. Craig Sanders, *Limiteds, Locals, and Expresses in Indiana, 1838–1971* (Bloomington: Indiana University Press, 2003). Information on the demise of Indianapolis passenger trains was gleaned from several sections of this thorough, informative, and well-written book.

5. Hetherington, *Indianapolis Union Station*, 58–59.

6. Ibid., 57. The summary of the preservation of Union Station that follows was drawn primarily from chapter 7 of Hetherington's book, which has a detailed account of this monumental effort.

7. Until the early 1970s, fireless steam locomotive #1, an 0–4–0 built in 1950 by Porter, switched coal cars at the power plant and is today at the Indiana Transportation Museum.

8. Study of this subject has even extended to what happens when communities lose their railroads—see Joseph Schwieterman's series *When the Railroad Leaves Town*, the first volume of which was published in 2001 by Truman State University Press.

9. Jeffrey Spivak, *Union Station Kansas City* (Kansas City, MO: Kansas City Star Books, 1999), vi–vii.

10. Sam Roberts, *Grand Central* (New York: Grand Central Publishing, 2013), 17.

BIBLIOGRAPHY

Books, Magazines, Newspapers, Pamphlets, Other Published Sources

American Railroads. Washington, DC: Association of American Railroads, 1953.

American Railway Guide and Pocket Companion for the United States. New York: Curran Dinsmore & Co., 1852.

Barrows, Robert G., and Leigh Darbee. "The Urban Frontier in Pioneer Indiana." *Indiana Magazine of History* 105, no. 3 (September 2009).

Bodenhamer, David J., and Robert G. Barrows, eds. *The Encyclopedia of Indianapolis.* Bloomington: Indiana University Press, 1994.

Bogle, Victor M. "Railroad Building in Indiana, 1850–1855." *Indiana Magazine of History* 58, no. 3 (September 1962).

Borneman, Walter R. *Rival Rails.* New York: Random House, 2010.

Bruce, Robert V. *1877: Year of Violence.* Indianapolis: New Bobbs-Merrill Company, 1959.

Burgess, George H., and Miles C. Kennedy. *Centennial History of the Pennsylvania Railroad Company.* Philadelphia: Pennsylvania Railroad Company, 1949.

Carper, Robert S. *Focus: The Railroad in Transition.* South Brunswick, NJ: A. S. Barnes and Company, 1968.

A Chronology of American Railroads. Washington, DC: Association of American Railroads, 1962.

The Cincinnati Union Terminal Pictorial History. Cincinnati: Cincinnati Chamber of Commerce, 1933.

Crump, Thomas. *The Age of Steam.* London: Constable & Robinson, 2007.

Dolzall, Gary W., and Stephen F. Dolzall. *Monon: The Hoosier Line.* Glendale, CA: Interurban Press, 1987.

Donovan, Frank P., Jr. *Railroads of America.* Milwaukee: Kalmbach Publishing, 1949.

Droege, John A. *Passenger Terminals and Trains.* New York: McGraw-Hill Book Company, 1916. Facsimile reproduction by Kalmbach Publishing, 1969.

Drury, George H. *The Historical Guide to North American Railroads.* Milwaukee: Kalmbach Publishing, 1985.

———. *The Train-Watcher's Guide to North American Railroads.* Milwaukee: Kalmbach Publishing, 1984.

Dunn, Jacob P. *Greater Indianapolis.* Chicago: Lewis Publishing Co., 1910.

Farrington, S. Kip, Jr. *Railroading the Modern Way.* New York: Coward-McCann, 1951.

Forty-Fifth Annual Report on the Statistics of Railways in the United States. Washington, DC: Interstate Commerce Commission, 1932.

Geib, George W. *Indianapolis: Hoosiers' Circle City.* Tulsa, OK: Continental Heritage Press, 1981.

Goldberg, Bruce. *Amtrak: The First Decade.* Silver Spring, MD: Alan Books, 1981.

Goodwin, Doris Kearns. *Team of Rivals.* New York: Simon & Schuster, 2006.

Hainesworth, Lorna. "Historic National Road: An All American Road." *Maryland Historic National Road* website, 2011. Available at http://marylandnationalroad.org/wp-content /themes/mnra/pdfs/Historic-National-Road .pdf.

Hanlin, George. *Historic Photos of Indianapolis.* Nashville, TN: Turner Publishing, 2006.

Harper, Glenn, and Doug Smith. *The Historic National Road in Ohio.* Springfield, OH: Ohio National Road Association, 2010.

Havighurst, Walter. *The Heartland: Ohio, Indiana, Illinois.* 2nd ed. New York: Harper & Row, 1962.

Henry, Robert Selph. *This Fascinating Railroad Business.* 2nd ed. Indianapolis, IN: Bobbs-Merrill Company, 1943.

Hetherington, James R. *Indianapolis Union Station.* Carmel, IN: Guild Press of Indiana, 2000.

Hilton, George W. *Monon Route.* Berkeley, CA: Howell-North Books, 1978.

Hipes, Steve, and David P. Oroszi. *Pennsylvania Railroad Lines West.* Hanover, PA: The Railroad Press, 2004.

Holland, Kevin J. *Classic American Railroad Terminals.* Osceola, WI: MBI Publishing, 2001.

Holloway, W. R. *Indianapolis. A Historical and Statistical Sketch of the Railroad City.* Indianapolis, IN: Indianapolis Journal Print, 1870.

Howell, Cecil G. *The Building of the Pan Handle Division of the Pennsylvania Railroad.* Privately published, 1995.

The Indianapolis Terminal, Bulletin No. 149. Swissvale, PA: Union Switch & Signal Co., May 1932.

Jackson, J. B. *Landscapes.* Amherst: University of Massachusetts Press, 1970.

Johnson, Erik C. A. *Reflections on America's First Union Depot.* Indianapolis: Erik C. A. Johnson, 1978.

Kostof, Spiro. *The City Shaped.* New York: Bulfinch Press, 1991.

Leary, Edward A. *Indianapolis: A Pictorial History.* Virginia Beach, VA: The Donning Company, Publishers, 1980.

Lewis, Edward A. *American Shortline Railway Guide.* Milwaukee: Kalmbach Publishing, 1986.

Lewis, Robert G. *Handbook of American Railroads.* New York: Simmons-Boardman Publishing, 1951.

Marlette, Jerry. *Indianapolis Railways.* Terra Alta, WV: Pioneer Press of West Virginia, 2002.

———. *Electric Railroads of Indiana.* Indianapolis, IN: Hoosier Heritage Press, 1980.

Meeks, Carroll L.V. *The Railroad Station.* New Haven, CT: Yale University Press, 1956.

Meints, Graydon M. *Indiana Railroad Lines.* Bloomington: Indiana University Press, 2011.

Middleton, William D., George M. Smerk, and Roberta L. Diehl, eds. *Encyclopedia of North American Railroads.* Bloomington: Indiana University Press, 2007.

Miller, Donald L. *City of the Century.* New York: Simon & Schuster, 1996.

Mitchell's Travellers Guide through the United States. Philadelphia: Thomas, Cowperthwait, & Co., 1836.

"New York Central Railroad." *Fortune* 20, no. 5 (November 1939).

The Official Guide of the Railways. New York: National Railway Publication Co., June 1916 (facsimile reproduction, 1979); August 1949; May 1950; June 1954; June 1962; July 1963; September 1964; August 1965; June 1968; May 1970; February 1971; April 1971; May 1971; June 1971; November 1972, July/August 1974.

The Official Register of Passenger Train Equipment. New York: Railway Equipment and Publication Co., 1971.

Ohio State Journal, February 25, 1850. Photocopy of newspaper page. No vol. or issue number.

"Organized Movement Demanded." Indianapolis *Sun,* February 18, 1910.

Public Timetables, various issues, 1945 to 1971: Amtrak, Chesapeake & Ohio/Baltimore & Ohio, New York Central, Penn Central, Pennsylvania.

Quiz on Railroads and Railroading. Washington, DC: Association of American Railroads, 1942 and 1947 editions.

The Railroad Gazette 43, no. 26 (December 27, 1907).

Railroad History, no. 137. Railway and Locomotive Historical Society.

Raitz, Karl. *A Guide to the National Road.* Baltimore: Johns Hopkins University Press, 1996.

Rand McNally & Co.'s Commercial Atlas of America. Chicago: Rand McNally & Company, 1918.

Rehor, John A. *The Nickel Plate Story.* Milwaukee: Kalmbach Publishing, 1971.

Rose, Linda C., Patricia Rose, and Gibson Yungblut. *Cincinnati Union Terminal.* Cincinnati: Cincinnati Railroad Club, 1999.

Rosskam, Edwin and Louis. *Towboat River.* New York: Duell, Sloan and Pearce, 1948.

Rybczynski, Witold. *A Clearing in the Distance.* New York: Scribner, 1999.

Sanders, Craig. *Limiteds, Locals, and Expresses in Indiana, 1838–1971.* Bloomington: Indiana University Press, 2003.

Saunders, Richard, Jr. *Merging Lines.* DeKalb: Northern Illinois University Press, 2001.

Scheiber, Harry N. *Ohio Canal Era.* Athens: Ohio University Press, 1969.

Simons, Richard S., and Francis H. Parker. *Railroads of Indiana.* Bloomington: Indiana University Press, 1997.

Sisson, Richard, Christian Zacher, and Andrew Cayton, eds. *The American Midwest.* Bloomington: Indiana University Press, 2007.

Smith, Thomas H. *The Mapping of Ohio.* Kent, OH: Kent State University Press, 1977.

Smith, William Prescott. *The Book of the Great Railway Celebrations of 1857.* New York: D. Appleton & Co., 1858.

Spivak, Jeffrey. *Union Station Kansas City*. Kansas City, MO: Kansas City Star Books, 1999.

Stilgoe, John R. *Metropolitan Corridor*. New Haven, CT: Yale University Press, 1983.

Sulgrove, Berry. *History of Indianapolis and Marion County, Indiana*. Philadelphia: L. H. Everts & Co., 1884.

Sulzer, Elmer G. *Ghost Railroads of Indiana*. Indianapolis, IN: Vane A. Jones Co., 1970.

Sweetland, David R. *Pennsylvania Railroad Color Pictorial*. Vol. 2, *St. Louis to New York City*. La Mirada, CA: Four Ways West Publications, 2000.

Taylor, George Rogers, and Irene D. Neu, *The American Railroad Network, 1861–1890*. Urbana: University of Illinois Press, 2003. First published 1956 by Harvard University Press.

Taylor, Jerry. *A Sampling of Penn Central*. Bloomington: Indiana University Press, 1973.

Transportation in America. Washington, DC: Association of American Railroads, 1947.

Travelers' Official Guide of the Railways, June 1870. New York: National Railway Publication Company. Facsimile reproduction, 1971.

Travelers Official Railway Guide for the United States and Canada. New York: National Railway Publication Company, 1968 (facsimile reproduction of June 1868 issue).

Vance, James E., Jr. "The American Urban Geography." In *Cities: The Forces That Shape Them*, ed. Lisa Taylor. New York: Cooper-Hewitt Museum, 1982.

Wallis, Richard T. *The Pennsylvania Railroad at Bay*. Bloomington: Indiana University Press, 2001.

Watt, William J. *The Pennsylvania Railroad in Indiana*. Bloomington: Indiana University Press, 1999.

Westwood, John, and Ian Wood. *The Historical Atlas of North American Railroads*. New York City: Chartwell Books, 2007.

Wilson, Jeff. *The Model Railroader's Guide to Trackside Structures*. Waukesha, WI: Kalmbach Books, 2011.

Young, David M. *The Iron Horse and the Windy City*. DeKalb: Northern Illinois University Press, 2005.

Manuscripts, Reports, Research Notes and Papers, Other Documents

Many of the following sources came from the Banta, Baldwin, and Indiana Historical Society collections cited below.

1877 The Belt Railroad and Stock Yards Company 1927 Golden Jubilee. Typescript, no author.

Articles of Association of the Indianapolis Belt Railway Company. Photocopy of typescript, n.d.

Conexus Indiana website. http://www.conexus indiana.com.

Hetherington, James R. "The History of Union Station." Paper presented at the 2003 Railroad Symposium, Indiana Historical Society. Archived at www.indianahistory.org.

Howe, Daniel Wait. "A Descriptive Catalogue of the Official Publications of the Territory and State of Indiana from 1800 to 1890." *Indiana Historical Society Publications*. Vol. 2, no. 5. Indianapolis, IN: Bowen-Merrill Co., 1886.

I.U. Ry. Co. Report of Original Cost. Typescript, undated carbon copy, William Henry Smith Memorial Library, Indiana Historical Society, c. 1922–1923.

Mendinghall, Joseph S. *The Beginning Point of the First Public Land Survey*. National Register of Historic Places/National Historic Landmarks Inventory-Nomination form, 1974.

Paxson, Frederic L. "The Railroads of the "Old Northwest" before the Civil War." *Transactions of the Wisconsin Academy of Sciences, Arts, and Letters* 17, Part 1 (October 1912). Available at http://www.catskillarchive.com/rrextra/abonw .Html.

Shank, Wesley. *Union Station: Written Historical and Descriptive Data*. Washington, DC: Historic American Buildings Survey, National Park Service, 1970.

Public and Private Collections

Brian Banta Collection: Indianapolis Union Railway locomotive photos and archival materials.

Indiana Rail Road Company Corporate Archives: Indianapolis Union Railway histories.

Indiana State Library: Historic Indianapolis maps.

Richard K. Baldwin Collection: Indianapolis Union Station timetables; ICC valuation records; Indianapolis and Union Station photos.

William Henry Smith Memorial Library, Indiana Historical Society: Indianapolis Union Railway and Stockyards Company Collection; Indianapolis Track Elevation Collection; W. H. Bass Photo Company Collection.

INDEX

Detroit, Michigan, 5, 7
diagonal streets, *6*, *7*
dining-parlor-observation cars, *47*
"Donation Line," 5
Downing, M. A., 123
DX tower, 130, 147, *149*, *150*, 176, 177

East Winds Bar, *174*
economic effects of railroads: on communities,
    20–21; prosperity, 19, 52, 75, 185; and Union
    Depot, 61. *See also* commercial/industrial area
    of Indianapolis
Electro-Motive Division of General Motors, 161, *163*
Elgin, Joliet & Eastern Railway, 122
Eli Lilly and Company, 181, 187, 209
engine house/machine shop, *127*, *172*, *173*
European immigrants, 77
Evans Milling, 187

Fairbanks-Morse and Company, 161, *162*, *163*
federal regulation of railroads, 187
Ferguson, James C., 123
Fordham, Elias, 5
"40 acres and a mule" expression, 16n4
freight: and Big Four freight house, 37; and birth of
    belt lines, 121–23; bypass tracks for, 69; and de-
    pots of railroads, 29; and Illinois Central Rail-
    road (IC), 208; of Indiana Rail Road (INRD),
    49; and modern train shed, *204*; and Monon, *48*;
    and original Union Depot, 63; of Pennsylvania
    Railroad, *189*; and Union Tracks, 161, 169; vol-
    ume of, *38*

gauge size of rails, 181n1
General Aluminum and Chemical Company, 187
General Assembly, *9*
General Motors, 186, 187

girdling trees, 4
Goodwin, Doris Kearns, 1
Grand Central (Roberts), 216–17
Great Depression, 112, 190
Great Lakes, 1
Great Railway Celebrations of 1857, 22, 27
Great Steel Fleet, 191
grid plan of American towns, 5–6, *6*, *7*

Harrisburg transportation Center, Pennsylvania, 69
Hawthorne Yard of PRR, 40
Heald, H. P., 93
Hetherington, James R., 65, 72
Holiday Inn and Crowne Plaza, 202, 215, 216
Holloway, W. R., 20, *30*, 51–52
Holmes, William C., 123
homesteading practices, 4
Hoosier Dome (later RCA Dome), *203*
Hoosier Heritage Port Authority, 207
Hoosier State, 207
hotels, 62, 70

Illinois, 2, 22, 25
Illinois Central Railroad (IC), xii; approach to
    Indianapolis, 49; and Belt Railroad, 146, 187;
    consolidations of, 32, 46; and control of India-
    napolis rail routes, 28; current state of, 208; and
    original Union Depot, 61; passenger service of,
    190; railroad mileage in Indiana, 46; routes of,
    46, 49; and track elevation, *85*; tracks of, *212*
Illinois Street tunnel: before and after photos of,
    94–95; converted to baggage tunnel, *91*, *92*, *95*;
    improvements made to (1888), 65–66, 79; and
    street/rail conflicts, 63, 73, 79
immigration from Europe, 77
Indiana: capitol of, *14*; dawn of Railroad Era in, 22;
    as nexus of rail routes, *30*, 51; railroad mileage

in, 25; rail routes of, *29*, *30*, *31*; statehood for, 2;
    statehouses of, 7, *9*; topography of, 3
Indiana, Bloomington & Western Railroad
    (IB&W), 32, 33, 35
Indiana, Decatur & Western, 45
Indiana Central Railway (IC): completion date
    for, 32; establishment of, 40; and Indianapolis
    Union Railway Company, 56; and joint tracks,
    56; and Terre Haute & Richmond Railroad, 40
Indiana Historical Society, 39
Indianapolis, Bloomington & Western Railroad
    (IB&W), 33, 124
Indianapolis, Cincinnati & Lafayette Railroad, 33
Indianapolis, Crawfordsville & Danville Railroad, 33
Indianapolis, Decatur & Springfield Railroad
    (ID&S), 32, 45
Indianapolis, Delphi & Chicago Railroad, 46
Indianapolis, Indiana, 1–16; and Central Canal, 12,
    14; challenges faced by, *198–99*; Common Coun-
    cil of, 56, 79; as Crossroads of America, 28; and
    early railroad construction, 51; establishment of,
    2, 5, 7–9; first railroad in, 20, 22, 28; and Inter-
    urban Era, 186; landscape of, 8; and Madison &
    Indianapolis Rail Road, *15*, 20, 23; map of, *132*; as
    nexus of rail routes, 51; number of railroads in,
    186; passenger service in, 190, 192; plat of, 5–8, *6*;
    population of, 25, 186; as "Railroad City," 28, 121;
    rail routes of, 28, *29*, *30*, *31*, 33; skyline of, 37; as
    state capital, *9*; as transportation hub, 11
Indianapolis, Peru & Chicago Railway (IP&C), 45,
    128, 130
Indianapolis & Bellefontaine Railroad (I&B): and
    advertisements for railroads, 23; and Cleveland,
    Columbus, Cincinnati & Indianapolis Railroad
    (the Bee Line), 35; completion date for, 32; con-
    solidation with New York Central, 33; depot of,
    54; and Indianapolis Union Railway Company,

122–23; completion date for, 32, 32; depot of, 52, 54, 121; as first railroad in Indianapolis, 20, 22, 28; and Indianapolis Union Railway Company, 56; and Jeffersonville, Madison & Indianapolis merger, 40; and joint tracks, 56; and original Union Depot, 61; and Peru & Indianapolis Railroad, 45; and population of Indianapolis, 25; and railroad fever, 20; route of, 28; tracks for, 59

Madison Railroad, 52

mail contracts held by railroads, 191

Main Street Station, Richmond Virginia, 67, 69

Mammoth Internal Improvement Act (1836), 12, 20, 45

Market Street, 7

Massachusetts, 21, 25

Massachusetts Street (later Avenue), 7, 33

Max Katz Bag Company, 187, 209

McCrea, James, 65

McKeen, William Riley, 123, 124

Meridian Street, 7, 72

Metropolitan Corridor (Stilgoe), viii

Michigan, 2

Michigan City, 11

Michigan Road, 11, 12

mid-Atlantic states, 16

Middleton, William D., vii

migrant traffic, 24

mileage, railroad, 22, 25

"Mile Square," 5, 6, 7, 29, 53

Miller, John F., 123

Milwaukee Road depot, Milwaukee, 67, 69

Milwaukee Road depot, Minneapolis, 67

Minneapolis, arched train shed in, 67

Minnesota, 2

Mississippi River, 1, 11, 22

Monon Railroad (Chicago, Indianapolis & Louisville Railway): and Belt Railroad, 124, 187; consolidations of, 32; and control of Indianapolis rail routes, 28; dining-parlor-observation cars, 47; fleet of, 47; freight traffic of, 48; *Hoosier*, 47, 115; nicknames/names of, 45, 46; passenger service of, 47, 190; route of, 45–46, 207

Monon Trail, 46, 207

Montgomery, Alabama, arched train shed in, 69

Monument Circle, 28

Moorefield Junction, 135

Morris, T. A., 56, 58

Mount Royal Station, Baltimore, 69

Muncie, Indiana, 33

National Interstate and Defense Highways Act (1956), 78

National Limited, 192

National Railroad Passenger Corporation. *See* Amtrak

National Register of Historic Places, 202

National Road (National Trail), 8, 11–12, 25, 27

National Starch, 187, 209

New Albany, 11

New Albany & Salem Railroad (NA&S), 45–46

New England, 16, 25

New Orleans, port of, 1

New Orleans steamer, 11

New York, Chicago & St. Louis Railway (NKP; Nickel Plate Road), 28, 45

New York Central Railroad, 33–35; and Belt Railroad, 154, 169, 175, 187; and Big Four Yard (Avon Yard), 187; and Chicago service, 22; consolidations of, 32, 33; and control of Indianapolis rail routes, 28; and freight traffic, 38, 169; Great Steel Fleet, 34; and Indiana, Bloomington & Western Railroad acquisition of, 35; and Indianapolis Union Railway, xii, 196; and Mohawks, 152, 153; passenger service of, 118, 190, 191, 192; and

Pennsylvania Railroad, 41, 187; predecessors of, 33, 35; routes of, 24, 33, 35, 112; stature of, 116; and timetables, 82–83

New York City, 22, 216–17

New York State, 22, 25

Nickel Plate Road (NKP; New York, Chicago & St. Louis Railway): and Belt Railroad, 187; and control of Indianapolis rail routes, 28; and interchange of cars, 177; passenger service of, 190; route of, 45, 207

Norfolk Southern Corporation, 45, 190, 209

Norfolk & Western Railway, xii, 32, 45, 207

North Carolina Street, 8

Northwest Territory, 1–2

Nowak, Ed, 37

observation cars, 47

Official Guide of the Railways and Steam Navigation Lines of the United States, Porto Rico, Canada, Mexico, and Cuba, xi–xii, 191

Official Railway Guide, xi

Ohio: dawn of Railroad Era in, 22; and Madison & Indianapolis Rail Road, 15; railroad mileage in, 22, 25; townships in, 16n3

Ohio, Indiana & Western Railroad, 33

Ohio River: and Baltimore & Ohio, 22; and National Road, 12; and New Albany & Salem Railroad (NA&S), 46; steam powered watercraft on, 11; and westward expansion, 1

oil house of Belt Railroad, 140

Olmsted, Frederick Law, 5, 7, 8, 53

opposition to railroads, 21

Pacemaker Freight Service boxcars, 37

packing business, 122

Pan Handle (Pittsburgh, Cincinnati, Chicago & St. Louis Railroad): and Belt Railroad, 136, 146,

JEFFREY DARBEE is a historic preservation consultant in Columbus, Ohio. He has written articles for *Traces of Indiana and Midwestern History* magazine and has authored books on a variety of historical topics.